BRAS, BOOTSTRAPS, AND THE BIBLE

STORIES OF RESILIENCE

Antoinette Allen, Ph.D.

Publishing Information
Bras, Bootstraps, and the Bible
Copyright©2019 Antoinette Allen
All Rights Reserved.

ISBN: 9781645506027 (Paperback)
Cover Design: Alaka Oladimeji Basit

TABLE OF CONTENTS

* * * * *

DEDICATION

For my family and friends, for me, and for my faith...

To my father, who told me—on the day I finished this book—that he never worries about me because he knows, "When life swallows you up, God will spit you back out in a rainbow."

Also, to my mother who worked tirelessly to convince me nothing could triumph over me. I finally believe you and thank you for giving the best of yourself so I could grow the best of *my*self.

In this book, I also write in honor of every little girl who knows deep inside of her, she is being called to greatness in big and small ways. To every girl growing up, never stop listening to your inner voice, despite what the circumstances or opposing voices may tell you.

To every woman of color who has wondered if her voice, vision, and experience truly matters: I assure you it does.

To every ally who helped me along my journey, I am forever grateful for your support and wisdom. And to every veteran who wants to tell their story...do it!

"*Growth does not occur until we have been pushed beyond our pre-determined boundaries.*"

Antoinette Allen

INTRODUCTION

As a woman of color, I have frequently traveled, turned, and stopped at the intersection of race and resilience. My life has been uniquely crafted in such a way that my race has not only increased my resilience, but also—at times—defined it. Let me just explain that I did not choose these building blocks; they chose me. This made it difficult to share my concerns with my peers, since there was a stigma and a subtle shame of raising race issues in a professional setting.

Reporting any offenses would often just put an unwelcome spotlight on an already deeply troubling matter—and so, for years, I suffered in silence. Nowadays, I would not do that; I have learned that asking for assistance does not make you weak; it makes you brave, capable and strong.

This book is designed to tell a story—since I consider one of my gifts to be storytelling—and to serve as a guide to building that great resilience within yourself; inside, you will find useful tips and tools to benefit you as you explore ways to both build it and celebrate it. I will also be sharing some of my most memorable military moments and lessons to help you along the way.

1

As I began to reflect on my military years, I could not help remembering spectacular veterans who had forever influenced and enriched my life. I still cannot say enough about the men and women continuing to dutifully serve this nation despite the trials and risks it brings. The next time you see someone who formerly served or is currently serving, please thank him or her, since there is no doubt they also had to gain toughness and resilience to do what they have done.

I am also forever grateful for the many civilians who tirelessly support veterans, day in and day out, many serving as surrogate parents in my younger days away from home, providing home-cooked meals and words of advice.

My military experiences helped make me who I am, but you can take my stories and apply them to your own chosen walk of life. You will get a clearer view of life for military women and see areas in which these life lessons can be adapted for you.

* * *

Everyone has a story and, according to my old theater professor, all good stories have a beginning, middle, and an end. This is where the title comes into play.

Bras, Bootstraps, and the Bible articulates my journey and gives but a glimpse into my personal resilience model. Your story is your own great source of resilience; no matter what, no one can take your story from you or make it theirs. It is your route to strength and fortitude, something that motivated me to ensure my children knew some of their mother's colorful military tales. I hope they help motivate you to reflect on your own heroic bra, bootstrap, and Bible stories.

Sincerely,
Antoinette Allen

CHAPTER 1

THE POWER OF THE STORY

As you already know from my introduction, twenty-one years of military experiences have taught me a great deal about people, life, and, most of all, resilience. Passing this wisdom along to others is one of my contributions to the world.

I believe I had the quality of resilience already, inherited from my parents and enhanced by certain life lessons when I was young, but it was the military that honed it, making me stronger, agile, and flexible. It tested my mind, might, and muscle, making me a better person, giving me purpose at a very early age and teaching me how to serve others. I am aware of what an honor it was to have given those years to my country—and I am thankful I did.

Resilience Defined

"Do not judge me by my successes, judge me by how many times I fell down and got back up again."
Nelson Mandela

As an educator and practitioner of leadership, resilience is currently one of the most popular topics. While it has many definitions, I define it as your capacity to keep moving forward during great adversity. Secondly, it means being available to move forward despite the fear and negativity beckoning you to stay still. Thinking in a motoring analogy, it is the fuel in your tanks; it gives you the emotional, physical, and spiritual energy to get to the next destination.

Even when we have fuel in our tanks, we can still learn new ways to increase it.

Resilience is a learnable skill, which means we have the capacity to discover and implement new behavioral knowledge to take us farther, and possibly faster.

Continuing with the motoring scenario, you may benefit from categorizing your past and current adversities in four simple categories: regular, mid-grade, premium, and diesel.

Recalling past situations that were low-grade adversities (regular or mid-grade gas) can provide insights and wisdom for your day-to-day future, while living through especially difficult situations (premium or diesel gas) prepares you to help others faced with similar situations.

All adversities give you a gas reserve to draw on later, and to share.

If the lyrics of the Rascal Flatts song, *Life is a Highway* are true, then we better ensure we keep our tanks full and that we are using the right octane level of gas!

The Birth of Resilience

When exactly did I become so resilient? At what point in my life did I tip the scale to find myself confident enough to know whatever I faced, I would be all right?

Well, I really do not know when it happened, but again, I am thankful it did.

As I have searched the pages of my life, I find my resilience story beginning very early in childhood. In fact, before I was even born, trouble was brewing concerning my arrival.

"Well-meaning" relatives were encouraging my mother to abort me. She was not married to my father, and in those days, having babies out of wedlock was considered shameful. I am so fortunate my mother was a resilient woman as well, who despite the shame and pressure she was facing, persevered and chose to have me.

I am also fortunate to have a father who continually reminded me that I was strong. I learned a great deal about loss from him, as my father is the only surviving sibling out of six children. All my paternal aunts and uncles died early, and this caused my father an enormous amount of sorrow.

Watching him attempt to recover from those losses has been difficult, yet he has been able to maintain his zest for life and uncanny sense of humor. Whenever we are together, you will find me giggling or laughing hysterically from some joke or wisecrack. I am fully convinced my dad uses his humor to continue to see the good in life.

Both of my parents credit my birth with maturing them and helping them to see beyond their selves. I've been told I came into this world with a bit of a fanfare, arriving with a bad set of tonsils and the umbilical cord wrapped so tightly around of my legs that it had cut off its circulation. Then there was the moment of shock at my arrival and the fact I was born covered in hair, which eventually fell off. I must have been all the rage in the nursery.

This may all explain why I have never minded standing out from the crowd. I entered the world unique and have embraced the reality of the fact there was only one *me* in all the universe.

One winter evening when I was six years old, I survived a very traumatic event which served as a baseline for my future coping skills. During bedtime, I heard my mother calling out my name. I must have looked in the living room to see what she wanted and saw the house was on fire. My instinct was to hide under the bed; fortunately, when my mother found me, we were able to escape before the house burned to the ground.

My mother recalls the front door on the house had been sticking for some time. It was difficult to open and often required you to fiddle with it for a few minutes before getting it to open. However, when she ran toward it on this night, it seemed to open by itself on her first attempt. When the door miraculously opened, I took my body and braced the door jamb with my hands and feet when the cold air hit, preventing her from safely taking me outside. I was literally trying to stay inside the burning house, because of the cold on the outside.

I can't imagine my mother's terror. What a moment for me to start acting up!

I recall as if it was yesterday, Aunt Carolyn standing outside on the porch, telling my mother to push me out the door and promising she would catch me. My mother did what she said and pushed me out into the night air and my aunt, sure enough, caught me.

I watched our home burn to the ground, sitting in the back of my granddaddy's old El Camino. I recall the fear, the curiosity of what would come next, and the sadness I felt, knowing things had changed and not being sure of what might happen next.

I believe it was on that day I was formally introduced to resilience and since then, it has been a constant companion on my life's journey.

I vividly remember my mother being so distraught and how my grandmother consoled her and told her how strong she was. While she was not speaking directly to me, she was unwittingly addressing something deep inside of me. I affectionately refer to this innermost sacred place as "spirit." You may be more comfortable with another term, but I believe every person has the essence of God securely lodged within him or her.

Sometimes it is hard to find, but you can be sure it is there.

Your spirit holds the roadmap to where you are headed, and can be trusted to get you there safely and on time. While watching our home being reduced to rubble and listening to my grandmother's spoken words, my spirit was interpreting the events for me. My little mind understood exactly what my grandmother meant when she elevated her voice to tell my mother, "Definitely, you will make it through this." I believed everything she said. I not only heard it, but felt it in my body and stood at attention, prepared to carry out her orders.

We did get through it, and the early trauma I felt prepared me for the path of difficulty lying ahead. I literally only had the clothes on my back, no shoes on my feet—but within a few days, our community had provided more than enough support for me to return to first grade in style. This experience created what I consider a very high resiliency baseline. For me, fear to the point of giving up must exceed the fear I felt hiding underneath my bed while the house was on fire. I have only encountered this a few times in my adult life.

I have lived a life using my grandmother's words as the cadence inspiring me to march on, despite my pain, fear, or disappointment. I have used the imagery of my mother moving forward as a portrait of what is expected. I still hear my grandmother's voice shouting, "You are strong, you will survive, and you will make it through this."

Despite those early setbacks, my body, mind, and spirit were steeped in an energy compelling me to move forward. This served me well for the most part, but did lead me to make some bad judgment calls in areas where I ignored my need for assistance. My newfound skillset caused me to handle some tough issues on my own when I should have asked for help earlier. Several of my resilience stories are tied to racial adversity and my attempt to overcome the negative emotions tied to them.

Antoinette the Resilient

When I teach someone about resilience, I ask them to write their name with the words "the Resilient" beside it, because I firmly believe our momentum rests in us seeing and thinking of ourselves in this way. Would you be willing to write your name somewhere on this page—or a sheet of paper—followed by the words "The Resilient?" Would you take another minute and say your name in this manner aloud? How cool is that? Weird, but it somehow has the potential to change the perspective of how you see yourself. Many people define resilience as, "the ability to bounce back after setbacks," but I want you to focus on bouncing back *better*.

After completing one semester in community college, I joined the U.S. Air Force. While joining the military was a great decision for me, it was not always an easy path. I left family and friends behind, and bravely moved halfway across the country. I was often the only woman and/or person of color on the team and certainly did not fit the military stereotype. I experienced obstacles and oppression while serving; nevertheless, the challenges molded me and made me stronger. I was determined to bounce back *better,* and often, I did.

A few years ago, I became very interested in capturing my voice and visions after I completed in-depth research on three women leaders for the completion of my doctoral degree. I was fortunate enough to collect the resilience stories of three senior-level black women leaders who held positions in the United States Federal Government. Each of these women had achieved the highest civilian position in their office. The research entitled, *When I See My Face: Painting the Portrait of Black Women Leaders in the United States Federal Government* focused on understanding how they each bounced back from adversity. I was curious concerning how they were able to remain steady while other leaders crumbled.

Bras, Bootstraps, and the Bible is an extension of my research as I attempted to document the inspirational portions of my life, these concepts being consistent themes keeping me successfully grounded. When I visualize this model, it is in the form of a triangle, in which *the Bible* is on the bottom line, as the foundation, while *Bras* is on the right, *Bootstraps* on the left.

Each section is dependent on the other to draw strength. The triangle has three sides, but each edge does not have to be equal. There can be three, two, or no equal edges and this is relevant when you chart your resilience path. While I have found the three main edges to my path, they were not equal at times or for different situations.

It is important to know which edge you are leveraging the most during your trial. It is also helpful to consider what and who else is available to assist you.

Forms of Adversity

There are several forms of adversity, but I have broken them into four types. While there are many others, I have attempted to place them into four major categories for easy identification. Knowing which type you are facing may prove helpful in seeking solutions. It's interesting to me how many people want to pursue being more resilient, yet they have not acknowledged this is an open invitation to difficult situations. Whether invited or not, adversity is a fact of life.

When I was young, my grandmother would often say, "Just keep on living." This was her subtle way of saying I had so much more to learn about life, and that my perspective at the time would change as I accrued knowledge with age. She was right, because life has been a great teacher and adversity has been a course I have continued to repeat.

Emotional Adversity

Trouble stemming from emotional wounds or current emotions in general.

Historical Adversity

Centered around historical issues. This could be past events you have no control over, yet you continue to be impacted by them. This is also relevant to circumstances you inherited.

Personal Adversity

Originates from personal issues, to include man-made and natural disasters. Events troubling the personal realm of your life.

Professional Adversity

Issues impacting your career, professional goals, or affecting the desired harmony of your workplace.

Resilience and adversity are a couple; they are dance partners. Consider which one is in the lead role on your life's dance floor. Most of my life, resilience took the lead, but there came a time several years ago when adversity was tired of following and moved center stage. It was very dramatic and unexpected, and before I knew it, I was dancing to a different drum. The music had changed in my life without me realizing it, changes creeping up on me, and it seemed the pace was faster than I could keep up with. The beauty of resilience, though, is that it's a fast learner, and once there was a pause, it was back in the lead. All along, my resilience was simply studying the circumstances, the rhythm, and waiting for an opportunity to be the lead dancer once again.

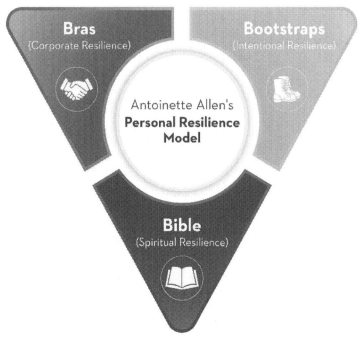

Be Who You Want to Be

Often when veterans tell their stories, they get asked if they are war heroes. What a great question, but in my case, the answer is "No". I am not a war hero, a POW, and I did not do anything meriting an award for heroism from the military. My story is the same as those of the countless veterans who often go unheard of or who are—unfortunately—forgotten.

Throughout the years, I have passionately shared my stories with others as I taught classes or mentored others, and these have nothing to do with heroism at all. One is not heroic just by serving.

I am the epitome of the average American who serves. You will not find any stories of me running through the desert, escaping, or trading gunfire with the enemy, but you will find common experiences you can relate to as you begin to think about your life.

I was just a small-town girl from the town of 'Nowhere Fancy', America, who began this amazing adventure that took her to places she never thought she would see. In fact, I was raised in Charles City County, VA a small town outside of Richmond, VA. As a child, I marveled at the trips to the big city of Washington, DC and never dreamed of the future places I would visit. I have had an amazing career and it continues to excite me. This experience—of leaving small-town life and seeing the world, of suddenly finding myself thrust into a new environment—really fires me up to show others that they can break their personal walls or confines and do something different. I love to encourage those who do not know what they want to do with their lives.

Let me assure you that this—not knowing what you want to do— is perfectly normal; most of us have junctures where we do not know what we want to do, simply knowing we must do something! These junctures can also come at any lifestage; people tend to imagine it's just something happening to the young. It isn't. Many people get partway through a career or a life decision, only to find it isn't working for them and they need a new direction.

How do you work out what (or who!) you want to be?

Start with what you are good at or passionate about, and if it still leaves you unsure, then start with something else—something that sounds interesting. I have learned where you start out is not nearly as important as where you'll end up.

I am simply encouraging you to get started on *something*.

You've probably also expected me to say this, but unashamedly, I would like to say the military is also a great option for those of you who are willing and able, even if you are a little unsure about it. The military mindset will soon make you determined to find your niche there—there are many of them to be discovered in the military—and to do a great job, whatever it may be. It will focus your mind and teach you skills you will take with you wherever you go in later life. You will be surprised at the doors it may open for you—mentally and practically.

The military and even government employment provides a unique opportunity to get skills to put you on the path of your desired destiny. I decided to put my past to use in a way to help others and I heartily encourage you to do the same.

Emotional Highways

There is no way to describe resilience and the path to increasing it without dealing with the emotions accompanying it. There is a vast array of these, yet four primary emotions will be most common to you; anger, fear, happiness, and sadness are primary emotions you are bound to feel. Think of those bright Crayola crayons you played with when you were a kid; there was the big box and then there was the smaller box. Remember those?

Well, this is one way to think of your human emotions. The next time you are feeling blue, think about *what shade* of blue it is—and why you chose that shade for the emotion. Just thinking of this will take your mind off your troubles, even if just for a few moments. This is the art of distraction and it works phenomenally to shift the trajectory of a negative thought pattern.

I learned to use this when my children were young and fixated on one object or process. I noticed how the quick introduction of another object or activity would change the atmosphere from a tantrum to swift and stable calm as they became engrossed in the new object or activity.

Personally, I've noticed this is effective for me as an adult as well. Naturally, the object or problem does not fully disappear with the introduction of a new thought, object, or activity, but the longer I spend focusing on the distraction, the less I dwell on the negative one.

The new one may also buoy my enthusiasm and self-belief and set me onto new paths where negativity is not able to be in control anymore. This discipline greatly enhances and accompanies the path to resilience.

Music, art, and nature can also assist you in moving from a negative emotional state to a more positive stance. If you're anything like me, music will play a major role in your emotional life and has a way of acting as a time machine. When I hear a song from my teenage years, somehow, I revert to the memory of that time and its accompanying emotions. This is beneficial when you need to strengthen yourself. Revert to a time when you perceived yourself to be strong or victorious and listen to that soundtrack to help you get through the current situation.

Not only do I use music, but I also lean toward art as another tool to communicate and shift my emotional states. In my doctoral work, participants visually described themselves using two images:

1. How they saw themselves, and
2. How others saw them.

I have replicated these numerous times and it is a powerful exercise; it evokes numerous emotions and is helpful to understand the differences in the two images, giving the individual an opportunity to decide if they want to bridge the gap between these images or not. You may do the same concerning your resilience.

1. Select one image representing strength or resilience.
2. Select an image depicting how you view your current strength or resilience.
3. Select an image depicting how you want your strength or resilience to look.

These visual exercises have the capacity to ground you when you feel weak and unsure of your next step, opening your eyes to see yourself in new lights. It's easy to get bogged down in self-reproaches, feelings of doom and gloom—and even outright telling yourself you're a failure, can't get to where you wish to be, and so on. This is negative self-talk and it is dangerous.

The negative voices wish to sidetrack and divert you from your self-esteem and your goals. There is another side of you that sees the positive and finds a way through, one that knows the best path to take and will lead you toward it. This is the voice you need to follow. Imagine pressing the mute button of the negative voices in your life and blasting the volume on the positive voices! As odd as it sounds, imagery is powerful.

What does the positive voice say to you? Fine, it may not shout at you very much, but it is there. His voice may be a little hesitant and trembly compared to the negative one, but visualize hearing it clearly more and more, and see your strength and certainty grow!

Several years ago, I was sitting in my corner office with its window, in a very rewarding position. Accompanying the portraits of my family were images which brought me joy or served as a reminder I could achieve joy. My office was highly decorative, and often people would comment concerning how inviting it was.

The walls of my office told tales of where I had been and where I was going. Of course, I was glad it had a positive effect on those who visited, but mainly, it was for my benefit.

I needed constant visual reminders of my existence and ways to remind myself that my journey was still evolving with adventures awaiting me. It could have been tempting to settle into the position and not realize what else was possible. I had military images to ground me to my past, sunflowers to display happiness, and an image of a boat in clear blue waters with the word "Destiny" in my direct line of sight. It was a scene from some island in the Caribbean.

When asked about the art piece, I would remark, "This is where I want to be."

Simply, it was my 'happy place', and sometimes when the stress was too much, I would shut my door and center myself by staring at the portrait.

I would imagine the warmth of the sun and the sound of the waves crashing onto the rocks. I starred at the boat and visualized myself rowing far away from the pressures I was facing. I lay on the beach and gazed upon the beauty of the ocean and the shore. After a few minutes of daydreaming, I felt relaxed. I could hear the steel drums and the imaginary song lyrics in the distance automatically making me sway. When I returned to my desk, I was smiling and ready to take on whatever awaited me.

This is an instant vacation and it can positively influence your outlook and your health. Not only did I do this personally, but also shared it with my assistant. She loved the beach, so I brought her a little bottle of sand and a beach photo frame. I told her to put a favorite photo of herself at the beach in the frame and place it on her desk. I also encouraged her to use this technique for stress relief. We had a good laugh, but we were both smiling when others were frowning and stressed.

As a woman of faith, I also had two key inspirational scriptures close by. I had a plaque on a shelf that read, "Be still and know that I am God." I read this nearly once or twice a day, because it was reassuring to confirm my job description did not include running the universe. It also provided a directive concerning how stillness is a viable option yielding tangible benefits.

Then, on my desktop in front of my keyboard was a small plaque stating, "Work unto the Lord." It quoted a Bible verse from Colossians 3:23-24. I needed a reminder that my reward would not come from humans, but a higher authority. It also kept me grounded when people's responses and gratitude did not match the effort I had contributed.

I knew I would always do my best and, equally, I would always know that it would be rewarded; the *here and now*, and whoever judged me at work, were not things I should worry about beyond striving to be the best I could be.

Someone Crashed My Happy Car

For several years of my career, I oversaw an administrative work unit. I had direct responsibility for twenty-five employees and indirectly supported over 100. It was an emotionally stressful position for me and taught me a great deal about traveling along emotional highways. This was the first time in my career I'd encountered personal sadness in the workplace, many things evoking sadness for me personally and professionally.

I felt as if I was fighting a war on two fronts, unsuccessfully, and it was the most difficult period in life for me. Nevertheless, what I learned during those years would prove to be priceless.

The combination and timing of events were overwhelming and began to affect my demeanor at work. I was fortunate to have a few allies in the office who held me together professionally while I was privately falling apart. I should have anticipated the chaos, because before I started this job, I had attended an office party.

When I was being introduced as the new Director of Administration, people gasped and one woman who had previously retired, grabbed my hand and lovingly said, "I feel so sorry for you." I was taken aback but smiled, laughed a little and—said nothing.

Wow! Talk about a missed opportunity to ask probing questions. I overlooked all the clues due to my optimism and zeal to take on the next level of leadership. As if that wasn't enough, the guy I replaced bluntly told me, "I have no doubt you will master the work of this job; you will probably find that part easy. It's people that are going to be your problem." I quickly shrugged his advice off thinking, "but people love me." How quickly I found myself retracting those words and accepting the truth of his wisdom. I was young and arrogant, yet this leadership experience humbled me and taught me valuable life lessons.

As a key leader in the office, I felt an obligation to look as though everything was fine. I did not have anyone in my chain of command who seemed remotely interested in the emotional tsunami destroying me. As the only minority leader, I was heavily scrutinized by employees and this put me under tremendous pressure. I was being internally crushed in the office daily and was finally realizing it was impacting my home life as well. In fact, when I went to my supervisor to tell him I had some personal issues to discuss, I had tears welling up in my eyes.

I was concerned about how I was going to explain it and to what level of detail, but all my concerns were averted. He never looked up from his computer and said, "Yeah, yeah, no problem, whatever you need." I felt numb knowing there was no compassion or care for me, but was also relieved I did not have to bare my heart to another person.

I'd been nervous when I'd entered his office, and momentarily relieved when I left.

Yet, this was another missed opportunity for us both. Had I received care from him, it would have served to build trust. Without it, I continued to remain apathetic concerning my leaders and their ability to see me as a person and not an entity. As a leader, I was disappointed. When people came into my office with their issues, I would listen empathetically and assist in any way I could.

However, when it was my turn in the barrel, my leaders failed me. There was no one above me to serve as a bra, but beside me were a few people who came to my rescue. No one above me noticed my puffy eyes from crying on the way to work or how my smile had diminished. If they did, they certainly didn't bother to inquire or offer to assist. This lack of connection tainted my experience, but simultaneously convinced me this was not my final destination.

Emotions play a key role in your ability to bounce back better. Your scenario, perceived loss, and the depth of emotion will influence your recovery and resilience efforts.

In my classes, I use the analogy of vehicles to explore emotions with my students. Vehicles and emotions take us on journeys and drive us to places. I also love to acknowledge the fact we also take others on rides with our emotions as well. Many of you can think of times it seemed as if you sat in the passenger seat of a vehicle that was being controlled by an emotion. I vividly remember my ride in the sadness vehicle; it was uncomfortable and foreign. The doors were locked, and at various points, I considered myself the victim of a kidnapping.

I had always ridden in a happy car. However, a few years ago, sadness pulled up, honked its horn, and whisked me away to a destination unknown to happiness. It was the fight of my life to switch cars, even though I knew I had to. Unfortunately, the only other cars offering me a ride at that time were fear and anger. Happiness really did not know where to find me, and I felt lost and hopeless. Even when happiness finally showed up, it was only for a quick ride; my main transportation was anger and sadness for at least three years. I write about what I know to be true, and I know what it is to travel on an emotional highway to a destination unknown.

I know what it is to have been historically resilient and to have it tested in a manner that causes you to wonder if weakness is your new normal. I also know it is important to take an inventory of it and your current emotional state to prepare for the road ahead of you.

Knowing what vehicle you are riding in is an important first step. Once you know what emotion is driving you, you can think about where it may be taking you. You should also think about where it has taken you in the past and determine if you enjoyed the ride.

Of all the emotions, anger was my least favorite. It was the fastest driver and made me feel out of control. Long-term anger was new to me and spilled out into every decision. Yet I would be lying if I said I did not enjoy riding in the vehicle a few times.

The situation I was facing would have made anyone angry and I felt I had a right to ride in the car, but if we are not careful, our anger can take us places we were never designed to go. I was reminded of this today as I walked along the beach picking up seashells. Among them was a toy race car, the perfect illustration of a vehicle being driven somewhere it was not supposed to be. I kept it and marveled at the damage the saltwater had done to its wheels and paint. Then I thought about the damage many of us have endured also from emotional adversity.

I usually used a monster truck to symbolize anger, but I think of the car I rode in as a fancy sports car. It was flashy, and I thought I looked good sitting in it, but the reality was that anger made a fool out of me. It is a dangerous vehicle to ride in long term and it changes you. Prolonged exposure to negative emotions will take a toll on you. My time with these new emotions has taught me valuable insights I would have never gained without them. I know I am a better person after I took a ride on the emotional highway, since I took away many observations while I was seated in the passenger seat. Eventually, something changed in me; I noticed it was a choice to remain in the vehicle or to get out. I had felt like I'd been kidnapped, but now I realized something; this revelation did not mean I should not try to escape.

Recently, I was teaching my youngest daughter how to handle her anger. I gave a very honest disclaimer, as this is a new emotion I too am learning to master. I started by assessing her anger and asked her, "How angry are you? Is it red or green like the Incredible Hulk?"

She replied, "Incredible Hulk," through her tears.

I said, "Ok, let's imagine we have a green box we are going to place your anger inside, because we can't let it keep you awake tonight."

She agreed and seemed to like the concept. I told her we would keep an eye on the green box and we did not want to give it to anyone else because it belonged to her. I assured her it would always be there in the box for her. Nobody would touch it or try to take it away from her. And it made the anger just a little bit fun, as odd as that sounds. Now, she knew it languished inside a box, waiting for my daughter to take a peek inside and decide whether she would free it.

This simple exercise really helped her to conceptualize her strong emotions and gave her a way to see how she was misplacing her anger toward her brother who had not wronged her. The one she was angry with was her father, but she had been hell bent on taking it out on her baby brother because he was an easy target. I held her close and patiently waited until she stopped being the Incredible Hulk and turned back into her former self.

The Original Wound

For as long as I can remember, I've enjoyed listening to people's stories. It was very early in my life when people began to share some of their troubles with me. Yet when I was young, I did not know what to do with that information, so I learned to listen and enforced that they were heard, offering encouraging words. I consider myself among a long list of storytellers; I never realized this gift came with a beacon to naturally draw people to me to share their own stories.

There were many instances where people would look at me after sharing something very personal and confess, "I don't know why I told you that." Not only do I consider myself a storyteller, I am very aware I am also a healer. At least, it is what I consider one of my main purposes in life. I am pursuing a path to help people to move forward.

I believe there are three distinct needs every person is in search of. We all long to be heard, seen, and valued; whenever one of these areas is violated, it is felt as a loss and creates a void that must be filled. In America, there was a well-known saying many of us grew up hearing, which served as the instigator for some of our voids. The saying was, "Children should be seen and not heard." This is the equivalent of putting an "X" across the first box and creating a deep wound which follows children into adulthood.

I have seen the effects of this in several of the adults I have encountered throughout the years, and these voids continue to wreak havoc in personal and professional settings. Each of us has a unique opportunity to try and fill those voids—or at least not violate them further with every person we encounter. The way we handle personal interactions with each other can heal each of these areas. I have had all three of these areas violated in the workplace, which led me to pursue coping strategies. I began to strategize how I might lift my spirits and considered the walls of my office.

I spent several hours a day in my office and sought to add inspirational images in my line of sight to inspire and encourage me. I realized I could influence my emotional state by the images and sounds surrounding me. I also spent several hours of my day mediating, resolving, and trying to understand the many behavioral quirks showing up in the behaviors of employees.

Often, there was a five-year-old boy or girl standing before me in an adult body. The original wounds, when unhealed, presented themselves in everyday interactions. I made myself a personal goal of not reinjuring people when possible.

Heard

Active listening is an excellent tool to use toward ensuring others feel heard when they are in your presence. This is the ability to clear your agenda and *be present* with the person attempting to communicate with you. It is the art of being fully engaged in the essence, movement, and rhythm of the conversation.

Seen

Acknowledging the person with whom you are speaking and reflecting what they said back to them is one way to make people feel seen. There is an African saying known as, "Sawubona." It is the intentional practice of letting others know they are equal in importance based on their humanity. It goes beyond them being seen; it is attempting to give them life by your recognition of them.

Valued

This is the most violated area for most people, because it is the most sought-after. Simple words of affirmation, encouragement, or gratitude are a few ways to help others know their value. Allowing yourself to actively find the value of every person you interact with will result in you noticing the many ways you are also valuable.

Every day, someone is having the worst day of their life; I wonder how many of those people you've walked past today? I try to smile and speak to everyone who crosses my path. I never know what they are experiencing or what they may be facing at their next stop. I can remember kind words, gestures, and smiles of strangers when I was in turmoil. They meant so much; they seemed to validate my humanity, and I try to do the same for others. It is especially my delight to speak to young people. My teenage daughter has been telling me since she was eight, most children do not like it when adults speak to them. "Mom, it is just weird," I can hear her say.

I just laugh and hold true to who I am and how I want to present myself in this world.

Recently, I was in an elevator in an office building, and a young man got in. He looked to be in his late twenties. When the door closed, I said, "Hello, how are you doing today?"

He looked at me a little puzzled and then he began to tell me he was not doing great; he had a lot of work stress and some home stress bringing him down. I smiled, nodded, and acknowledged his willingness to share and wished him well. His stop was before mine, and before he got off the elevator, he looked back at me and thanked me for asking him and allowing him to get it off his chest. He seemed lighter, even though I do not know how long the feeling lasted.

I just know there is one less person in the world who could say, "No one cares about me."

CHAPTER 2

BRAS & THE POWER OF 'CORPORATE' RESILIENCE

"My mother said to me, 'If you are a soldier, you will become a general;
if you are a monk, you will become the Pope'; instead, I was a painter,
and became Picasso."

Pablo Picasso

I consider support systems to be the first key to my resilience, and I affectionately call them "Bras." I also refer to them as a type of 'corporate' resilience, where many hands, hearts, and heads are working toward a goal or project. This does not only apply to the workplace.

It just means that in this case, it is not you successfully mastering your current adversity alone. 'Corporate' means there is a body of people behind it, or, a collective of some kind (be that of people or other things).

In the corporation, all hands are on deck to assist, encourage, and provide you support during your time of need. Create yourself a list of those who stand ready and prepared to help in a time of great need—at work, and personally. And even if people are few in number for whatever reason, and no matter how short the list is, note you are never alone; the "bras" in your life—even if not people—may be found in a variety of sources to include memory and inspirational writings. In my case though, some of my bras are indeed people.

I met some of my best bras in the military, including my best friend, Lydia. She has stood by my side in every situation and crisis for the past twenty-five years. She is one of the few people in the world who have permission to tell me when I am wrong without an elaborate explanation. Everyone needs a few of those people in their lives. Do not limit your pool of potential "wisdom bearers", and know they come in large and small packages.

Several years ago, I was faced with major adversity surrounding the birth of my second child. I sat in a hospital room with my then ten-year-old daughter and husband, while the doctor stated, "You are going to have a baby today," to which I responded, "No, I am not."

I was only thirty-six weeks along and while the doctor had previously told me the baby's lungs were fully developed, *I* was not ready. How could the baby possibly arrive when I still had so much to do in preparation? The doctor looked at me puzzled and repeated himself, and then looked at my husband for reassurance. My husband could not provide him assurance or support concerning the matter either. He knew I had dug my heels in the sand and I was not prepared to have the baby right then for two very important reasons: one, the nursery was not ready, and two, my hair was not done. Back me up on this one, ladies. Whatever would the pictures look like?

I had another month, I thought, and I was scared because I had already suffered four miscarriages previously and could not bear the thought of losing this child too.

In the failed and angst-laden negotiations, a heroine arose in the form of my ten-year-old daughter who walked over to me, looked me in the eye, and firmly stated, "Mama, you are going to have a baby today and everything is going to be ok." My daughter was the wisest person in the room; she sensed the fear and uncertainty looming in the air and addressed it head on. The adults were offering knowledge, but she was offering wisdom. She projected a future state for me by telling me, "everything is going to be ok." I needed to hear those words in the simplest of terms, and she had painted a future outcome I needed to see in the present.

This technique is crucial when helping others through difficult times.

I was stunned. My doctor heaved a sigh of relief, and I looked at him and repeated what my daughter had just said as if it was my original idea. I am happy to report on that day, nine years ago, I welcomed another beautiful baby girl into this world and into my heart. This is the premise behind 'corporate' resilience, knowing there is a team of professionals (big or small) working on your behalf to get you what you need. People in your life can not only give you the factual details, but also the added assurance everything is going to be alright.

This is the benefit of having a talented team to aid you along your journey.

When I was first learning about bras, my grandmother taught me some key lessons concerning how to wear them and select them—but ultimately, way ahead of that time, my family served as my first bra. So, what is a bra? Bras support your breasts and serve as a protective cover; they also shield your heart by design. Over the course of my life, I have figuratively and literally had several bras. I have had sports bras, military bras, special occasion bras, and even went with no bra at times. Reflecting on the bras I no longer have has given me keen insight into the art of remembering. There are few bras we have the privilege of maintaining for a lifetime.

I would imagine very few of you still have your first bra; it probably does not fit you any longer or is worn out. This happens with the people who come and go in our lives as well. There are many bras that come to mind who no longer support me for various reasons. As you grow and change, so do your bras and the support selections available to you.

As I encountered adversity, I found the support that bras provided was critical.

I was able to draw upon the wisdom and lessons taught and gleaned to help me through some of my most difficult situations. Life will provide numerous opportunities to improve upon your resilience. Adversity has taught me countless costly and valuable lessons. I did not sign up for any of these lessons, but I do not believe I would have been taught them any other way. Even if I had, they would not have been as memorable as they were.

I have a long history of wounds and scars resulting in an incredible number of past obstacles I can look back at. Looking back at these events gives me confidence to weather future episodes. I encourage you to make a list of the things you have survived in your past. This analysis will help you to find strength to make it through your current situation.

This exercise was effective and eye-opening, to say the least. I had forgotten some of the stuff I experienced during the years and some of the bras I wore during those times.

Writing can be cathartic, especially about the past. I highly recommend it as a way of remembering how you became the person you are and as a means of celebrating your wins.

As a teenager, I worked all through high school as a waitress at Shoney's. This job taught me patience, dedication, and hard work. I worked with the most delightful women who took great care to make sure I went further than they did. They were nurturers who shared their struggles and told me I would not stay there after high school. Back then, it was good money, and having cash every day was the best. The older waitresses warned me not to get too comfortable with fast money because this was what had kept them waitressing. Every time I visit a Shoney's, I picture the younger version of me, and I smile seeing how many opportunities I have enjoyed after taking some sage advice from my former peers.

One of my former co-workers explained she had become accustomed to the daily cash, and since she was a single mother, she could not wait for a bi-weekly check, so she felt stuck. They encouraged me to go to college or get another job once I graduated high school, and with her words in the back of my mind, I was determined to stop waitressing when I graduated.

I am thankful for the care and guidance these women gave me at an impressionable age, and since then I have always had a special place in my heart for waitresses. These women were an extension of the hard-working women in my family and solidified my work ethic. The lessons I learned at Shoney's translated perfectly to my first military assignment as a customer service specialist.

You Are Too Pretty to Join the Army

"I have seen all the works which have been done under the sun and behold all is vanity and striving after wind."

King Solomon

Let me apologize to the many beautiful Army sisters for what may feel like an insult. It is merely a direct quote swaying my original decision on whether to join the Army or another branch. Often, I am asked, "What's the best branch of service?" This is a very deeply personal question for every member of the Armed Forces. My husband's answer is always the United States Marine Corp with an added, "Ooh-rah" battle cry for sound effect. My answer is, "The Air Force."

However, I did not know this when I joined the military, because I started all my qualification testing with the Army. I was clueless when it came to understanding what the roles of the individual military services were and I did not discover the existence of the Coast Guard until several years later. I was most familiar with the Marines, because in high school I spent my freshman year involved in the Junior ROTC program. This short stint as a Marine cadet convinced me I was never going to be tough enough to be a female Marine.

My husband and former high school sweetheart went to the Marines right after high school. He graduated one year before I did and after reading his letters portraying his basic training experience, I was fully convinced I was not Marine material. When I decided to join the military, the Army was the only other branch coming to mind. I called a recruiter and, immediately, they began the process. I went to the Military Entrance Processing Station (MEPS) with the Army and decided against that too, after a series of inconsistencies.

I received my first speeding ticket on the way to a Prince concert (so, worth it).

The recruiter told me not to worry about paying it, because I would be in basic training before my court date and the judge would just throw it out. I felt very uneasy about this and opted not to follow his advice. He was teaching me to be unethical. I considered that strike one, then he promptly shifted into strike two by showing me his pay stub and telling me, "Look at how much money you are going to make." I knew this was a lie, because he had a higher rank and a longer time in service than I would start with.

All of this left me very suspicious of the process and the Army in general.

The straw that broke the camel's back was the job they offered me at the Military Entrance Processing Station (MEPS). The entire process left me feeling as if I was at a used car lot. Everyone was peddling some offer and when you did not accept, another level boss would appear to give his or her sales pitch. I was not falling for it; I wanted a job in the medical field, and was determined to get it. I had been at MEPS all day waiting for a job offer, and when they finally offered me one, the Sergeant came out and offered me an 'opportunity' as a truck driver.

I stood in the middle of the MEPS floor with my hands on my hips, offended and declaring boldly, "Do I look like a truck driver to you?"

There was a group of soldiers gathered, pressuring me to sign, and then they began to laugh. I was serious and did not find the humor in the situation. Back then, my imagery of what a truck driver was did not match the former cheerleader standing in the room. Let me clarify something for you, concerning me. I was the last person anyone expected to go into the military, as I was free-spirited, very artsy, and eclectic. The only thing military about me was the combat boots I wore as a fashion statement alongside my dresses. Therefore, the military in general was a stretch, but being a truck driver was absurd to the younger version of me.

Even to today, my mother still looks at me and says, "The military is the last place in the world I thought you would ever go." Over twenty years later, I look back and think the same thing, but I do not believe I would be the woman I am today if it were not for those years I spent and the skills I amassed in the military. Exposure to amazing opportunities at an early age taught me valuable life lessons. I learned responsibility, accountability, and the necessity of service beyond one's self and loved ones. Those pillars set a foundation which has served me well. I want to instill those in the next generation through my writing and directly through my legacy.

After the recruiters realized I was serious, they started coming back with other offers. They began with the "What do we have to do to get you to sign today?" This was the end for me with the Army. I hate sales tactics and genuinely despise high-pressure ones. I was no dummy and knew what I was being told was a half-truth, and those recruiters were not looking out for my best interest. I learned early in life that a half-truth was a whole lie and began planning my exit strategy. I explained I would only be open to a medical position.

The Sergeant made a last-ditch attempt and asked, "If I offer you a guaranteed medical job, will you sign today?"

I thought about it for a minute and said, "Don't the people who collect the dead bodies count as medical?"

He reluctantly said, "Yes."

"Goodbye," I retorted.

Honestly, I was disappointed, because I had begun to imagine the possibilities of a military life. When I left, I went to visit my best friend. As I was venting, his mother overheard me, and she told me she had been in the Army Reserve years ago. She looked at me and said something that changed the course of my life.

"Brace yourself," she said. "You are too pretty to join the Army."

This caught my attention and I was all ears. Now, I know this could be highly offensive to all my sisters in the Army. Stick with me; I do not believe she meant it in the form of outward beauty only. I think it was her way of saying "This kid is in for a rude awakening."

She encouraged me to look at the Air Force, I think she knew me well enough, and as I said earlier, I was the last person anyone thought would join the military from all outward appearances.

I was a bit of a fashion rebel and did not conform to rigid rules. I incorporated my old ROTC combat boots as part of my fashion regimen. Looking back, I was weird and did not fit into any cliques at school. I was friends with all sorts of people. She went on to explain, she saw too many young girls joining the military with career aspirations, to only end up being married quickly or demoralized because the Army environment was very difficult for women at the time. Many women who served in the early days of military service have confirmed this. There is tremendous pressure to conform to the mostly male environmental norms that it has historically proven difficult for women to be authentic.

Well, despite what lay beneath her compliment, it was how I became aware of the Air Force and began perusing it as an alternative. I reached out to an Air Force recruiter and was in for another rude awakening in a different way. While the Army was nearly stalking me to join, the Air Force had a "take it or leave it" approach. The recruiter was hilarious! The first day I met him, he was recovering from a vasectomy. He told me this in order to explain the ice pack on his lap and his intermittent squeals of pain. Despite this, he was pleasant; he told me he would pull my scores and let me know what jobs were available.

He called me later in the evening. With a sense of urgency in his voice, he said, "Antoinette, I have something very important to tell you. If you are ever driving on the road and your car begins to make a funny noise, I want you to stop the car immediately, get out of it, and call a mechanic. Promise me you won't touch a thing."

"Ok," I said shyly.

He laughed and said, "You have the lowest mechanical scores possible, but you can get any other job in the Air Force you want, due to scoring high in the other categories."

I wanted to leave as soon as possible and did not want to wait for a medical job, so I selected the "open administrative" category, which guaranteed me administrative work and could later turn into a medical position.

When I began to backpedal and try to negotiate a better deal, he did not flinch and abruptly said, "I do not need you to join my Air Force; I have met my quota for the next two months. I have people lined up who want to come in."

He pulled out a stack of pictures of young people and began to tell their stories. He told me their names, what jobs they selected, and when they were leaving for basic training to prove his point. I was impressed and knew this man could care less if I joined—and that only made me want to join even more. His product was good, and it would be an honor for me to be a part of his organization. The Air Force did not need me; I needed the Air Force to get me to the next level. He had shifted my perspective and I was now convinced this would be the right move for me.

The recruiter practically escorted me to the door while exclaiming, "When you're serious, give me a call."

"What a different sales pitch," I thought. "Man, I have got to find out more about the Air Force."

I decided to join, and on May 20, 1993, began my remarkable journey.

Off We Go into the Wild Blue Yonder

"The power of an Air Force is terrific when there is nothing to oppose it."
Winston Churchill

I will forever be influenced by serving in the United States Air Force. From the traumatic nature of basic training to the realization that it was time to retire, I greatly enjoyed being an Airman. I went from a rebellious teenager one day, to voluntarily agreeing to let strangers called drill instructors tell me what to do and when to do it. I arrived on a bus in the middle of the Texas night only to find a less-than-inviting reception. A man with a large hat screamed at me to keep my hand on the handrail as I walked up the ramp. Then he got close to me and said, "Get it right, go do it again and hold the handrail this time." We were all dazed and confused and concerned about what was coming next. We did not have to wait long to find out, because when we got inside the building, there was a welcoming party ready to explain.

One of the first things the Air Force taught us was their theme song, "Off we go into the Wild Blue Yonder." I had no idea what it meant, but I understood I was going somewhere wild I had never been before. It was a wild ride, but I met some of the most interesting people one could hope to meet. I really liked the melody of the song and it was a moment of solidarity for the troops; it was something we all owned. Our unique theme song was the only music available to us outside of the 5 a.m. "Reveille" making my stomach turn.

I have never been an early riser and being woken up to the sound of the bugle every morning was traumatic. Not only were you rising before the sun, but also you were expected to be on the track and ready for the morning run. I have never been a runner and had significant anxiety every morning, trying to keep up with my squad.

Upon arrival, I was placed in a group of thirty women. This grouping would be called a flight and we would train together for the entire six weeks of basic training. We may have arrived as strangers, but we quickly learned to form alliances in order to survive. I was hating life and did not think I was going to pass basic training because of the running. I think I failed my time every day—except the day it counted most. It was the day of the test and I was nervous.

I had fallen behind as usual and could see my squad mates up ahead of me in the distance. There were two more laps left and something on the inside of me urged me to catch up with my flight and keep running the last lap. I had never done this before as my normal pattern was to catch up to them at the last lap and always be the last one across the finish line. However, this day was different, and I had a serious urge to get in the middle of the flight and stay there, so I did. It was fortunate I did because this day, the flight was running slow, and as the last person crossed, it was the last second anyone could pass.

If I had done my normal pattern and stayed in the back, I would have failed and been forced to stay another week or two. I firmly believe God was watching over me and had given me the urge and strength to persevere. I could not believe it and I am sure the drill instructors were shocked, because they had watched me fail every day before. I was truly doing my best, so when they would scream at me to pick up the pace or run beside me yelling, it had never made my legs any faster. Yet, I was motivated on the physical fitness test day to finish with all the bras that had been on the journey with me; I wanted to finish strong.

I can still hear me motivating myself as I had to sprint to catch up with them, saying "this is your last time doing this; you can do it, keep going."

This was the beginning of a series of cultural indoctrinations that were unwanted and unwarranted. Another of those moments found me in my second year of the Air Force.

I had recently been assigned to Seymour Johnson AFB and I was excited to be back on the East Coast, putting me closer to family. My adjustment should have been smooth, because I was a standout employee at my first duty station—Whiteman AFB—in a good way.

At my new unit, I was under intense scrutiny because I was working too fast. The girl I replaced was the office favorite, but where it took her six hours to complete a task, it took me three hours and then I would ask other sections if they needed help. My boss's boss did not seem to like this and told my newly minted supervisor to keep me busy even if it meant sweeping the floors. I did not take his comments kindly since I was the only minority in the workspace. I assured her I would not be sweeping floors, as no other person from the team swept floors. I tried to help her to see the optics and what I deemed as a slight.

What I did not know was there were major racial issues in this unit prior to my arrival. Later that month, I received a call from my former boss from Whiteman AFB with a warning. He warned, "Be careful, because they called me trying to dig up dirt on you and I told them you were the best Airman I had." He told my boss he found it hard to believe I would be stirring up any trouble. Not the answer they were looking for and I continued to work in what was my first hostile work environment until I was moved to another squadron. This move was a blessing to me, even though the unit had labeled three of us as troublemakers and abruptly reassigned us.

Little did they know that the team of "troublemakers" made them look ridiculous because of the great work we did in the Transportation squadron. I received numerous awards to include the Airmen of the month more than once while assigned there. You can imagine the look on my former supervisor's face during the presentation. It's funny to think of how many times people really believed they could harm me or tarnish my name with their unjustifiable motives.

There were several occasions when the harm was deliberate and many when it was merely an unconscious bias on the part of others. When I was first commissioned in the military, I noticed if I was with a male officer, people would salute him even if I was the higher-ranking officer. In the military tradition, you salute the officer with the highest rank first. I had become accustomed to this and one day mentioned it to one of my white male peers. He looked at me weird and I said to him, if you don't believe me, just pay attention for the next few minutes.

We were in a busy area at lunchtime, so we were going to pass several people. Over and over, Airmen would say, "Good morning, Sir," and they would salute him and never look at me. The problem was I was the highest-ranking officer and after the third person doing this, my peer stopped the last Airmen and in a very frustrated tone, he asked, "Do you see the Lieutenant?"

The poor Airmen looked confused and said, "Yes, Sir." Then why didn't you salute her instead of me? What a great question, but I had to pull my peer off the ledge and advise him to take it easy. I only wanted him to notice it, but once he did, it angered him.

This goes back to the original wound of not being seen. Well-meaning people erase you daily by not acknowledging your presence earlier. This taught me to make myself visible when necessary and to use my superpower of invisibility to my advantage.

During those times of not being seen, I gathered intel. I learned in my moments of invisibility to be a student of people by watching their body language. I connected the organizational dots and leveraged this knowledge at other times. People marveled at what I knew, and I am sure they wondered how I knew it since they never saw me.

Invisibility can be used to your advantage.

Black Girl in the White Man's Army

"When I was in boot camp, a drill sergeant saw me running across the field and he yelled at me, 'What's a black girl like you, doing in this White Man's Army?"

Iyanla

Let me begin with a clarification: I do not believe the military belongs to any person or race. It is an organization made up of diverse people. I have only used such a pejorative assertion to describe the U.S. Air Force based on my first expressed interest in joining. A black male soldier scolded me for my choice due to the lack of diversity by saying, "Why in the world would you join the white man's Army?" I did not know what he meant until much later.

This was the early 90's and the Air Force was mostly all white and male. I am not the only woman of color who has heard this expression while serving in the Armed forces. This may seem like an unfair proclamation to some of you, but it was an accurate portrayal of my military career at that time. I spent many years of my career advising senior leaders on the need to diversify their teams. This was often not a well-received message with one commander directly asking me, "What's wrong with the white guys I have?"

Much of the negative rhetoric shared with me about military personnel was proven untrue. I spent over twenty years in the military and met some of the most wonderful people on the planet. I have found them to be selfless and unrelenting in protecting their brethren and fellow citizens. I have not, however, found them to be perfect, because perfect people do not exist. In many minority communities, the preconceived notions continue to exist concerning what will happen to their sons and daughters if sent into the service. I can remember one elderly black man expressing genuine concern for me when he saw me in uniform.

I was surprised his impression of the military was one evoking fear. Yet, this is understandable when compared to the treatment his generation saw after serving in WWII.

I was always very proud to wear my uniform and particularly loved it when little children would stare. I wanted little girls and boys (especially of color) to see the possibility of military service in their future. It is vital for children to look up and see people who look like them doing positive things such as serving their nation. There are too many negative images of minorities and it was good to provide a counter-narrative of what patriotism looked like. I can still recall the moment I realized I loved this country and wanted to serve its people.

It was fourth of July 1993 and I was standing in full uniform at a military appreciation event with my basic training unit. The song, "Proud to Be an American," was playing, followed by a fireworks display. As I stood there, the gravity of the decision I had made to serve the country sank in. I was willingly agreeing to give my life to defend the Constitution of the United States of America. I became very emotional in the moment and was so proud to have the opportunity to do what many women of color had been denied the right to do before me.

My perceived race and gender provided the training ground for most of my early resilience training. My family did not tell me my skin color or being born female had any power to define me or limit me. The outside world soon attempted to instill that in me, but I was defiant to the assertion. I used the word "perceived," because according to my DNA results from both parents, my ancestry origins are 50% European, 49% African, and 1% Asian. I personally have always felt connected to every human being, despite race. Personally, I believe race is merely one puzzle piece of a person's composite. It is not the only piece and is certainly not the most important. This is a very personal assertion and I share this with you because it is critical to my journey.

I was the darkest child in my family on my mother's side growing up, and until my cousins started pointing it out, I was not aware of it. They were much lighter than me and would often tease me for my skin tone and hair texture. My grandmother would tell me to ignore them. Ignoring was the first step in my initial resilience regiment and it worked—until it didn't.

In my life, whenever I noticed inequality, I fought against it. I was determined I would not be limited by anything; if I wanted to pursue something, I did. It was the reason I became an officer in the military. As I looked at the pictures on the wall, I did not see anyone who looked like me. The lack of diversity in leadership and the ranks was deeply disturbing to me. When I was enlisted and expressed to someone that I wanted to become an officer, they told me they did not want any black officers. I asked them if someone told them this information or were they just assuming.

Their response back to me was I should look around for the answer.

I said, "Well, I'm going to finish my degree, apply, and see if they want me or not."

When I did look around, I only found one black female officer and she appeared to be very isolated, due to the overwhelming numbers of her officer peer group being white male and her female peers being enlisted. While they went to the Officers' Club in the evening to bond, she went to the gym alone. The military does not allow enlisted personnel and officers to socialize together, so this black female officer could not hang out with us. I used to look at her and see the sadness in her eyes. This made me even more determined to become an officer. I wanted there to be more diverse faces to see, I wanted to be a source of inspiration. By the time I became an officer, the sadness accompanying the solo status experience was long gone. I was accustomed to being the only person of color or the only woman on the team.

Personally, I refer to this phenomenon of being the only minority on the team as, "The Highlander Effect." I define it as the solo experience or status attained by a person due to the known identity marker in a group or team setting. I based this off the 1986 British film, "Highlander." The fantasy film depicted battles between immortal warriors. Whenever one warrior killed another warrior, the survivor would shout, "There can be only one."

This is the type of diversity and inclusion I have endured most of my career, inside and outside of the military. I do not say this as if it is a good thing. It can be very lonely and ultimately leaves you with fewer internal allies than one would have wanted. It also sets employees up to behave more as rivals due to the lack of cultural understanding.

I have often imagined the leaders of the organizations wielding their swords and shouting, "There can be only one!" I have certainly said it myself on numerous occasions as I looked around the office in wonder of how there were several minorities who could inwardly declare this catch phrase. This leads to dissension in the ranks and psyche.

Unfortunately, I have seen the chaos and friction taking place when another immortal warrior joins the team and the two begin to do battle for the solo spot. This typically happens with women and minorities. In America, you will rarely see white men battling for a spot based on race, because they continue to be the majority in several organizations. However, when other identity markers are applied, they can fall into this phenomenon easily.

I think this rivalry exists after learning to adapt to a culture and carving out a niche of identity, to find it threatened when another person who appears similar joins the team. For example, when there is only one woman leader, and another is chosen, you would like to think this would not be a source of tension. However, I have seen it become brutal, aggressively competitive, and petty at times. The woman joining the team is often unsure of what is happening and why her co-worker feels threatened by her presence. What happened to the welcome wagon? The newcomer has no insight into how her peer shifted her identity or how hard she worked for acceptance and, now this could be threatened by the new addition. This is a sad phenomenon, but it exists.

Instead of the Highlander Effect, I wish to share an alternative solution a former commander, Lieutenant Colonel Sanders, adopted in dealing with the new homogenous additions to the team. This commander fought to ensure I became a commissioned officer and she served as my mentor. There were very few female leaders in the unit, and she enjoyed mentoring us as we came through the unit. I remember her sharing an insightful lesson about a younger female officer who joined the unit. I greatly appreciated her mentoring, because she genuinely cared about my future and because she taught through story.

To explain the phenomenon, she used "cats" instead of "immortal warriors" as I did. She referred to herself as the "old cat" and the new officer as the "new kitty." She explained she had been around a long time and nothing she did anymore was cute, but the new kitty can get away with murder. The new kitty could pee on the carpet, scratch up the furniture, and no one would be upset, because that was just the sweet, new kitty. A hilarious analogy evoked images in my mind and easily conveyed how overlooked she felt. My commander was not bitter or jealous; she remarked she remembered her time as the young kitty and was happy for the next generation of female officers coming through the door. She was excited about mentoring the new officer but was the epitome of watching a young cat and an old cat interact. The old cat does not get flustered easily and does not get annoyed as the playful kitten explores its surroundings.

Highlander Effect	The Principle of the Two Cats
Creates a polarized environment	Creates an inclusive environment
Undermines team cohesion	Unifies strengths and perspectives
Pride	Prudence
Solo Status	Social Status

I operate a consulting business called "Two Cups of TLC" and I teach my clients to visualize two cups, which represent the two different perspectives we may sip from in any given situation. We may sip from a cup of bitterness and war, or a cup of harmony and peace. If possible, I encourage you to choose the latter cup. I have tasted each of them and can tell you only one of them will benefit you when you are trying to increase your resilience. I can also tell you only one leaves your breath smelling sweet. So, choose your cup and its contents carefully.

In the earlier days of my career, there were glaring racial disparities and treatments in general surrounding race. One included a restaurant that did not want to serve me lunch (while in uniform) because of my race. This is not an assertion; it's a fact. The server told my white boss, "Stop bringing those people in here." This was the first and only time I ever saw him angry. He apologized to the team and told us never to go there again.

But it wasn't her hesitancy to serve people of color that shocked him, it was her refusal to serve military personnel. In fact, my indoctrination to my first duty station was shocking and depressing. I sat in an auditorium with all new arrivals to Whiteman Air Force Base

(AFB) awaiting the in-processing brief to hear a white male Sergeant proclaim, "Welcome to Whiteman AFB. If you are not white and not a man, you will not enjoy your time here."

Most of the room broke out in laughter, while I sat there thinking, "Oh no, two strikes for me: I'm not white and I'm not a man." This was just the beginning of my Midwest indoctrination.

I knew what racism looked like only through the lens of living in Virginia, but Missouri racism was different. I was further enlightened when I got to my unit and met my first permanent supervisor. I will never forget that day; Staff Sergeant Latter introduced himself to our team with another racially charged set of declarations. Our team comprised three Airmen: one white male and two black females. Our new supervisor was a white male who—with no smile on his face— proclaimed, "Hi, my name is Sgt. Latter and, yes, I'm a redneck."

I instantly had an internal reaction and wondered what it could possibly mean. I knew what it meant back home and it was not comforting to me or the other black female on the team. We looked at each other in wonder and then he went on to clarify.

He said, "Let me explain what it means; it means no, you cannot take leave during hunting or fishing season because I will be on leave and it means if you screw me, I will screw you harder."

He went on to explain his philosophy of teamwork and his expectations. Despite my early concerns, he was one of the best supervisors I had in my military career. He created a wonderful professional environment and had a knack for inclusion.

Our close-knit team took care of each other and we were high performing.

Sgt. Latter shared his racist upbringing and former beliefs with me; the military had changed his belief system. He realized, inside, people were the same and had the capacity for good and evil and he credited his military exposure with opening his eyes and heart. We would laugh as he shared he had to pretend to be racist when he went home to visit his family in the South. His brother-in-law was a black man; he really liked him but could not show it for fear of ostracism.

Group mentality and peer pressure can persuade rational people to go against their basic instinct and morality. He felt he needed to pretend to be racist in order to maintain acceptance by his white male family members. While this was his sad reality, we chose to laugh about it. I have often used humor to mask my pain and it appeared Sgt. Latter was doing the same.

I have thought about him and wondered if he found the courage to speak his truth. I wondered if he returned home after he retired. I wonder, too, if he continued to pretend to be a racist or, worse yet, returned to being what I call an environmental racist.

The Power of 'Bros'

"There's nothing worse in this world, than a trifling woman."
Grandpa Jones

Throughout my life and career, there were not only women who cheered me on, but men as well. My path to resilience is laced with encouraging words and memories from several *bros*. My confidence began early in life due to the motivation I received from my grandfather. He believed I was destined to do something great and made me believe it was true. When I would come home complaining after school, he would tell me, "Baby, you got to get your lesson."

Education was priceless, as he and my grandmother did not graduate high school.

That was normal in the south for people of color, but he was determined I would know the value of education. He is the reason I have a Ph.D. behind my name today, because he instilled in me a love for learning early in my life, pointing me toward the value of being curious and I became a lifelong learner. He provided me some of the most interesting insights and lessons.

My grandfather was also my best friend growing up; wherever he was there, I was in tow. My grandpa had a glowing sense of humor and made people laugh; it is one of my cherished memories surrounding him. Often, when he was about to leave, I would ask, "Pop, where are you going?"

He would reply, "To see a man about a pig."

I never knew what that meant why he needed to check on the pigs, but it always caused me to giggle. He was critical in shaping me into the woman I am today, even though he died when I was fifteen. He was the first to tell me *what did not kill me, would make me stronger*.

He helped to uncover one part of the resilience path for me and I am so grateful for his guidance, influence, and love.

I did not think I would ever stop crying after he died. I cried so hard my eyes were swollen shut. I was spending the weekend with a friend from school when I got the call; I was distressed. I still remember running into my grandmother's arms when I arrived at their house, and I remember his empty spot at the kitchen table. For years after his death, when I walked into my grandmother's kitchen, I expected to see him sitting there. It took years before I could bring myself to sit in his chair. I could not imagine my life without him, and even into my adulthood, whenever I dream of him, it is always in reference to me looking for him and finding him alive. In the first fifteen years of my life, he shaped my view of the type of woman I would become; he told me he saw greatness in me, and I believed him and set out in the pursuit of that greatness.

I want to take a pause here and ask you what are you speaking into your children's lives?

Are your words charting a path for them toward destiny or destruction?

It is a valuable use of your time to stop to reflect about this, because your words and actions are stepping-stones for them to follow or trip over.

My grandfather had a vision for the type of woman he believed I would be, and he was careful to ensure I knew what the boundaries were. Fiercely protective of women and with a real distaste for domestic violence, he believed a real man would never lift his hand to hurt a woman and had no problem confronting the men who did. When I was a little girl, he told me, "Toni, there are only two types of women in this world: the marrying kind and the other kind. You will be the marrying kind. Do you understand me?"

I nodded my head in agreement, although I had no idea what he meant. However, as I got older, his words provided an imaginary boundary for me.

There have been wonderful men who have poured into my life throughout my journey. I like to refer to them as a "bro" instead of "bra," out of respect for them. They have supported, guided, and held me together during critical times in my career and I am forever thankful. One of the best decisions I ever made was to join the United States military and this decision is due in part to a bro. I wish I could tell you it was inspirational, with some wonderful words of wisdom, but it is not remotely close to the circumstances surrounding my decision to join the military. I have often been ashamed to admit it, but the truth is that I literally needed to get out of town. I honestly perceived my life was in danger and the fastest way to get out of Dodge was the military.

I had been thinking about enlisting prior to this situation, but this series of unfortunate events solidified it for me. After high school, I got my first apartment with my friend. My mother warned me moving in with my best friend would ruin our relationship, but I was young and thought I knew better than she did. I learned a valuable lesson: listen to your mama. The first few months went well; her boyfriend and I were very good friends in high school, and we all got along. The problems began when they broke up and she moved in her new boyfriend without my permission.

He had just gotten out of jail and we did not hit it off, my best friend caused a great deal of the tension between us. Looking back on this situation, I realize she was in over her head and did not know how to break things off with him out of fear.

My friendship with my roommate had deteriorated to the point she was providing fuel to ignite this young man's fire, frequently telling him lies to make him think I was not paying my half of the bills. I assume this was to get him to give her money, but it made him hate me. When he would confront me, I never knew what he was talking about and he was blaming me for dirty dishes I had not used. The truth was she would have her ex-boyfriend over during the day while this man was working, and when he came over in the evening asking why the kitchen was dirty, she would blame me. I was the pawn in a very dangerous game and my mother had not raised a fool.

Once I realized what was happening, I began an escape plan.

I was not initially afraid of him despite the altercations and words we had exchanged. However, this all changed when I overheard him telling her he was going to physically assault me when he caught me by myself. Instead of trying to defend me or shield me from harm, she was telling him to be quiet, because my grandmother was in the house visiting and she did not want her to hear what he was saying. Talk about the strap breaking on what I thought was a good bra.

I was agitated I had gotten myself into this type of drama. Anyone who knows me well, knows I despise personal drama. After that day, I decided it was best never to be at the apartment by myself. I did not know him well enough to know if he was serious, but I decided not to stick around to see if he would make good on his threat. The situation escalated quickly and went from rude comments and questions to verbal threats. I no longer felt safe at home, and since my roommate and I were no longer on speaking terms, I was required to act.

One day, I was packing my things and he came home, running up the stairs to confront me, only to find my father standing in my doorway ready to greet him. The look on the young man's face was priceless. It was as if he had seen a ghost; he backed up and even asked my father if he needed help. This incident was frightening, but it was the last push I needed to leave my hometown and begin my military adventure. I called my recruiter and asked for the quickest date possible to leave. This was adversity, if I had ever faced it, and I was terrified.

I reached out to my support system immediately and sought help to remedy the issue. I called a few of my bros for this situation and realized the importance of having a diverse network of people who genuinely care about me in times of crisis.

Lastly, I must tell you about my husband who has been a key supporter for most of my military years. There are several stories I could share, but I will share this one because it clearly articulates a level of care best described as astounding. He certainly earned the distinction of #1 Bro for this act of kindness. When I arrived at Squadron Officer School, I was not in the best shape physically and was not prepared for the Alabama heat or for running in it. I failed my preliminary run which meant if I didn't pass the retest, I would be sent home. I was worried, I had never failed a formal military event, and I was ashamed. It was a combination of my physical condition and the environment. I never adjusted to the heat, and eventually was diagnosed with asthma.

I called my husband in tears; I was panicky and unsure if I could pass the run in the next few days. He told me I would and offered to assist. I told him not to worry, since a few of the guys in my squad had agreed to run with me to help and would work with me during the days leading up to the run. He would not take no for an answer, however, and against my wishes, two days later he drove from Virginia to Alabama, just to set the pace for my run.

He ran alongside of me telling me to pick up the pace when needed and continually motivated me. I promise you there was no way I was not going to pass the run since he had gone to such great lengths to support me. Almost every military memory includes my husband standing beside me cheering me on. I will forever treasure the moment we crossed the finish line. I was floored by his support and his willingness to literally go the extra mile for me.

CHAPTER 3

BOOTSTRAPS: THE PURPOSE OF INTENTIONAL RESILIENCE

"If wealth was the inevitable result of hard work and enterprise, every woman in Africa would be a millionaire."

George Monbiot

"It's all right to tell a man to lift himself by his own bootstraps, but it is cruel jest to say to a bootless man that he ought to lift himself by his own bootstraps."

Martin Luther King Jr.

The second most important key to overcoming adversity is bootstraps. It can also be thought of as intentional resilience, the type you manufacture within your mind, power, and will. By bootstraps, I mean the ability to be able to pick yourself up. The bootstrap mimics the soul of a person. This type of resilience relies on your abilities alone and I have deemed it intentional, since it is typically the first place people gravitate to, trying to troubleshoot and self-diagnose their problems, looking for solutions. I encourage this also but caution you that you may not be able to handle everything on your own. It is helpful to have others assist you even in the early brainstorming phase of recovery. Thoughts formulated in your mind, actions implemented by your will, and strategies reliant on your emotions all reinforce your ability to use your bootstraps.

There is a common American phrase, "Pull yourself up by your bootstraps." It has been in use for over a hundred years. Over time, the meaning has shifted. Some used it to denote an improbability. Laced with sarcasm, it was merely describing a fool's errand to think someone could use bootstraps to pull their own self up. Somehow, the meaning of this statement became lost and in its place was an interpretation and directive for people to follow. A directive meant to inspire courage and perseverance. Not only was it not impossible to accomplish, but it quickly became an expectation and a measure of one's internal will. Americans proudly boast of their bootstraps and tell tales of how they overcame adversity by relying on them.

Grit, heart, and strength are tested when you have been sucker-punched or received a devastating blow. But there is no shortage of stories about the resilient and how they leveraged their bootstraps with one hand tied behind their backs. This leads many to attain a false sense of reliance on one's self, something which can sadly reap deadly consequences.

Putting too much emphasis on the bootstrap can lead to isolation and an overly independent existence. By my estimation, the bootstrap is an aid, not a levitation device. It alone does not have the power to lift you off the ground and I am hesitant to recommend the bootstrap as a stand-alone resilience strategy. It is *one* strategy that, when well-applied, can create an inner strength and confidence which cannot be shaken. If overused, on the other hand, it will lead you to acquire a false sense of self-reliance which will disappoint you in crucial times.

Whether you know it or not, you are the star of this drama known as "life" and there are some things you must do for yourself. Each of us gets to decide if we are going to produce and share our stage and spotlight with a full cast or not. For several years of my life, I was producing, directing, and starring in a one-woman show. I am proud of the accomplishments I achieved during those times, yet I realized my greatest times of fulfillment were when I was working with others. Growing up, I watched a network of women sit around a kitchen table discussing the affairs of life.

As a young girl, I saw this community as the natural rhythm helping to soothe, comfort, and make decisions. However, I did not mimic this model when it came to my problems. I chose to make executive decisions and rarely sought counsel. While others continually sought my advice, I sought myself, opting for those bootstraps every time until they failed me.

There will be many times and situations requiring your actions and decisions. This has the capacity to evoke quite a bit of fear and has resulted in some scary moments for me.

My independence has led me to operate in the "bootstrap" realm more often than necessary.

At an early age, I learned to rely on my capabilities and myself. While this makes me comfortable, it is not always wise, and it is not always possible. I see it now, with hindsight.

There are many times I should have sought the counsel of some bras or the wisdom of the Bible. Instead, I used my bootstraps to pull myself up. I thought I was putting on my "big girl panties" and decided to go back in the ring for one more round. In the back of my mind, there was a soundtrack of uplifting music spurring me on toward victory.

While I had successful outcomes, I more than likely took the long way around more than one time, due to my stubbornness and pride. I am a fixer, enjoying a challenge as well. This combination can make the bootstrap an attractive option when adversity hits, but beware. The three components are best when used together. When you overuse one component, you will come to rely upon it and it may let you down when you need it most. Inevitably, I came across some situations I could not handle alone. In those moments, I realized the bootstrap alone could not pull me up; it was the momentum of wanting to get back up on my feet with my boots in place.

Any way you theorize the "bootstrap" metaphor, it always leads you back to the understanding of self-reliance, and while I agree it's a necessary skill to master, it is not the most important one.

'Country Core' Values

> *"I learned the value of hard work by working hard."*
> *Margaret Mead*

Core values are a common set of ideologies the military ascribes for each member to memorize, live by and exude. I did not have to wait for Uncle Sam to give them to me; my family had already taught them to me. The elders in my family spent time instilling core values I continue to cherish today. I am fortunate in that what they taught me, translated well with what the Air Force expected.

This made it easy to achieve alignment with the Air Force's organizational expectations.

I consider the values from my early life as my 'Country Core' Values.

I was raised in a rural area of Virginia with a slow, yet whimsical pace of life. There were no streetlights, no malls, and lots of open fields. I think back on those days now with a hint of jealousy about how laid-back the days seemed compared to the pace of my children's childhood.

The lessons I learned in childhood have followed me into the workplace. For instance, my daddy taught me to treat people with kindness even on their worst days. He told me, "Never kick a dog when it is down." This nugget has come in handy on more than one occasion. It provided me an enormous amount of compassion that translated well into many of the positions I have held. I spent a bulk of my career in roles where I interviewed complainants, mediated disputes, and gathered witness statements. I was often face-to-face with disgruntled employees due to working in a variety of customer service settings. I got to see people at their worst and most vulnerable in several of the positions, and used the empathetic statement my dad suggested as a baseline marker for how I handled them, even when they were kicking me.

I learned to treat everyone with dignity and respect from my maternal grandmother, as she was tender-hearted toward people and had a unique ability to make everyone feel valued and special. She loved to bake and seemed to know every family member's favorite dish, delighting in fixing it for them on holidays or birthdays. I learned the value of studying people from her; she always knew what to say to bring comfort or a smile to my face.

I vividly remember the hug she gave me the day my grandfather died. I cannot remember the words she spoke, but I can still feel her arms around me and her fingers wiping my tears. All this, despite the fact she had just lost her husband.

I had an affinity for spending time with the elderly as a child. I preferred their company and the colorful tales they shared. I did not mind listening to their stories and found they were willing to listen to mine. When I was five, I decided I was going to run away.

I have no idea what I was protesting, but remember I got the idea from something I saw on a television show. I informed my grandmother of my plan and she seemed to understand. She never got rattled too easily by children's issues and always had a smile to share. She was indulging me as she patiently listened to my complaints about living at home.

She just asked me to eat lunch first, since she had already fixed it. I agreed, but not before packing a knapsack with a few things in it. I told her I would stay to eat, but I would leave when done. After I finished eating, I set out down our dirt road and walked to the end of it. At the house on the corner was one of the older women I would visit with my grandmother, sitting on the porch in a rocking chair as I passed by. Of course, my grandmother had called her to tell her I would soon be coming up the road. When she saw me, she asked where I was headed, and I explained I was running away. She smiled and suggested I come in for a Popsicle, because it was a hot day.

I sat with her for a while, telling her my plans as my little feet dangled from her gliding chair on the front porch. It is funny to think about how differently this scenario would play out with my children. There is an unfortunate reality concerning the network of little old women waiting to catch children at the corner, since this no longer exists in many neighborhoods.

During my adult years, I have not known my neighbors well enough to call them and ask them to entertain a potential runaway child.

I am unsure of how much time had passed, but before long, my grandfather was pulling in the driveway to pick me up. He told me my grandmother had told him I had run away, but he was there to take me back home. He was not mad; he just laughed it off and explained what my grandmother had fixed for dinner and he was sure I did not want to miss it. I was not sure how long I was supposed to run away for, but Pop made a convincing argument for going back already.

I went home, where I was greeted with a hero's welcome from my grandmother, who unpacked my knapsack. I never imagined running away again, and we laughed together as we told my mother about the day's events.

I am the first woman in my family to serve in the military, but not the only one who wanted to. Nannie, (my step-grandmother) used to tell me stories of how she wanted to serve during WWII, but they would not accept her because she was a mother. Nannie was the toughest woman I knew, and I learned a great deal from her about perseverance and sticking to your guns, no matter what. She was a vibrant woman, filled with laughter. It was a desire of her heart to help the country, so she went on to find some work to support the war effort. The way she described her younger patriotic self, intrigued me and planted a seed in a little girl, which grew into my military career.

Somehow, because she had wanted to serve the country, I thought I could, and I did.

Her stories painted a picture of women belonging in the military—a place where many thought women of color certainly did not belong—and one day, I inserted myself into that image.

And so, I ask you again: what type of pictures are you painting for the young people in your life? What images will future generations paint and insert themselves in because your stories and words made it possible? I continue to model this by inspiring my children with clear imagery of what is achievable to those who dare to believe, and to those who don't fear falling, because they know they are equipped to get back up, either unaided or by the power of bras or bootstraps.

Working in a mostly male environment changed the way in which I operated. It changed some of the original country core values I learned from the women, growing up. I did not discover this until years later when I began to work with mostly women. I accepted a position after leaving the military that unknowingly challenged my gender diversity skillset.

There was a way I had learned to communicate, behave, and lead; it was masculine in its nature. Since I had worked mainly with men, I assimilated to the culture; most of the military women I knew did also. This did not serve me well outside of the military environment, and in order to be an effective leader, I had to change my ways. I had to tug on those bootstraps once again in order to prepare for what was coming next in my life. I was intentional in leveraging the entirety of my value set to pave the way for my newfound authenticity.

Integrity First

> *"There are two things in this world that you don't mess with: another person's money and another woman's man."*
>
> *Grandma Jones*

Integrity is a hallmark value and can be found in thousands of companies' values, logos, and mantras, but it was also found on my mother's parenting checklist.

The fastest way to get a punishment in my childhood was to tell a lie; this was intolerable and was an early life lesson my mother reinforced at every opportunity. Since I prided myself on being a good girl for most of my childhood, there are very few memories of corporal punishment.

My mother offered an option between a spanking or a lecture. I would always ask for the spanking, thus precipitating her lecture instead. However, one night, I demonstrated a sheer lack of integrity— leading to a spanking! This was major, because my mother did not give an option; she came home and told me to prepare myself for a spanking the next day.

The women in my family had a rule: you never disciplined a child when you were angry. While this is advisable, it also prolongs the agony of the child who must wait for the punishment. It was torture, but well-deserved in this instance.

My cousin and I were at a community dance with our parents, and we were having so much fun. Around 8 p.m., our parents thought it was time to go home, but our mothers wanted to stay. Our stepfathers decided they would bring us home and let our mothers hang out a little longer.

The problem was my cousin and I wanted to stay and dance some more, so we came up with a strategy to ensure we could go back to the dance. I do not remember which one of us came up with the lie, but we told our stepfathers there were some men interested in our moms, and we bet that was why they wanted to send us home early and how unfair we thought that was.

How in the world did two little girls turn into deviants over the desire to dance to Michael Jackson so badly, we would risk telling such an outrageous lie? I have no idea what we were thinking, but I can promise you my days of lying and fictional narrating were over. Our stepfathers did not take us home; they took us to our grandparents' house and headed back to the dance. We knew we were in big trouble, but had no way of pulling our stories back, and since they were persuasive and confirmed by each other, they were deemed credible by our stepfathers.

This may explain why I am so sensitive to this subject, because it was a critical lesson, I learned the hard way. I have a real distaste for liars and lying; my children know the punishment for lying is much more severe than for the wrong they committed. I have tried to instill the appreciation for the truth from a very early age. I have erroneously assumed when an agency has integrity listed as a core value, the employees make every effort to align themselves with the value. However, I was sadly mistaken on several occasions.

When I joined the military, I had no concept of what it would be like or what would become of this time. I delighted in every pleasure it brought me and reconciled every pain I felt.

It shaped who I am today. My biggest disappointment was typically tied to discriminatory practices and attitudes I encountered. One of my favorite jobs in the military was training soldiers and Airmen on equal opportunity. I was surprised, one day, when two white male soldiers requested to speak to me after the training to inquire why I said they could not be members of the Ku Klux Klan and the National Guard.

Initially, I thought they were kidding, but they were serious. With a straight face, I explained they could not swear to defend the Constitution of the United States against all enemies, foreign and domestic, and at the same time bear allegiance to an organization holding values running opposite of the military's core values for all soldiers to be treated with respect.

They looked at me confused, and I looked back at them with empathy as I further stated, "I am in no way suggesting to you that you shouldn't be a member of the organization, I am telling you in accordance with DOD policy, you can't be in both."

I often think about the irony of the day and the emotions running in all of us, yet we had what was a very respectful dialogue. I learned, early in life, to mask my true emotions in order make other people comfortable. I do not recommend this; I am only sharing this to convey how I remained calm and this allowed me to engage in difficult conversations.

I think there is something to be said for building racial resilience at a young age. It forces you to create an identity that will withstand whatever the future throws your way. A significant amount of my early resilience-building came in the form of racial resilience. Everywhere I turned, I was faced with my brown skin causing a problem for someone else.

I mean, literally, the skin color God chose seemed to usher in opposition.

I vividly remember my first racial heartbreak. It was the summer before I went to 7th grade. I moved in with my aunt and uncle for the school year, until my mother could move to the new town. My aunt and uncle were fair-skinned and were often presumably white until I moved in. I became best friends with the white girl across the street. My family had a pool, so she and her brother came over almost every day.

We had a great summer, yet one day, she came across the street with tears in her eyes and said, "We can't be friends anymore."

I was scanning my mind and wondering what I could have done to her. I asked her, "Why?"

She stated, "My stepfather told me to tell you and your family to go back to Africa and jump up and down on your sticks."

I was so naïve, and I remarked, "I don't have any family in Africa."

We agreed to be friends at school, but we were no longer able to socialize outside of school. I did not understand what any of this meant, but the giant Confederate flag flying over their house took on a new meaning.

The new reality shattered who I thought I was in the world. I was raised in a very diverse family and was loved by all shades of people, so I was not prepared for the words from across the street. Yet, those words were merely precursors to prepare me for the 7th grade and beyond.

Later in the year, I went to church with my aunt to discover several of my white classmates and their families were there. As I waved to my classmates, their family members were gasping and whispering, "I think she is in the wrong church." I was the only brown body in the church; little did I know I was breaking Virginia protocol. See, the black church was located behind the one we were visiting, and once again, no one was the wiser my aunt and younger cousin should be deemed unwelcome until I joined them. Dating back to slavery, there were rules to how black and white parishioners worshipped separate or apart.

I was supposed to be out back in the black church, but since it was the late 1980's and not the 1880's, I was unaware of the rules. I will forever remember the look on the faces of the senior citizens in the church, staring at me with scowls. I wasn't equal to their grandchildren; I certainly was not a child of God. I was black and not welcome in their church. They made it crystal clear, and as I sat in the House of God hearing about His love, I wondered who really believed the message. I was in the house of hypocrisy, where my classmates were too afraid to speak because the watchful eyes of their parents were condemning them. I sat there continuing to smile at them, understanding the divide existing in the world and even in the church.

Well, Sunday was over, and Monday brought the same kids speaking and smiling as if nothing had happened yesterday. Maybe the episode in the church had disturbed them as much as it disturbed me, but I would never know because there was no apology or acknowledgement of my wounds or hurt feelings. This would be a repetitive pattern in my relationship with racial inequality.

Service before Self

In the first few months of being in the Air Force, I was faced with a very painful reality of an old stereotype of black women. My military career was marked with several traumatic racial incidents. While "integrity first" is a core value in the Air Force, I found many instances of individuals not living up to those expectations.

When I was in technical school, there were international students also on base. One Friday, we were riding the bus back to the dormitories, and one of the international male soldiers came and sat beside me on the bus. He said in broken English, "Hey baby, how about tonight?"

This came from out of nowhere; I smiled politely and said, "What?"

He leaned in closer and repeated himself and the laughs from the back of the bus began as his friends were listening.

I was stunned and nearly speechless, but found a few choice words to share with him before he left. All my friends were appalled and began to question me about why he chose to ask me. I did not know, but by the time we got off the bus, I was blood mad. When we began walking back to our rooms, one of the male international students came over to apologize. He explained they were told American women were easy—and black women the easiest of them all.

You can imagine how his apology went over, and while he was not the one who offended me, I did not have kind words for him either.

"Who told you that?" I asked.

He simply replied, "The American men."

How could my fellow Airmen, who professed to exude integrity, have betrayed us? How could they have thought so little of us who wore the same uniform, took the same oath, and served the same nation? Who gave them the right to speak of my sexuality based on my skin color? Over and over, I found myself faced with situations in which I had to choose service over self.

I chose to keep going despite my emotions because of the mission ahead of me and because it was what I had been taught to do. I'd been taught to be strong in the face of oppression and opposition. I'd also been taught to anticipate it, which I did to some degree but still had not quite expected to be verbally accosted by a soldier on the bus.

After basic training, most people attend technical schools, in which you learn the basics of your job. In nearly every military school, there is a distinguished honor known as the Honor Graduate; it is essentially the valedictorian of the class. When we were given our introductory brief, the professor explained the person with the highest-grade point average would be named Honor Graduate and the second highest would receive the Distinguished Graduate Award (DGA).

Throughout the course, I had the highest test scores. On the day the professor announced the awards, he stated another classmate would be receiving the Honor Graduate and I would receive the Distinguished Graduate Award. My peers, to include me, looked confused, because our test scores were not a secret. I did not say anything because the student the professor named was a white male and the instructor's favorite.

I was warned inequality existed, and this was certainly not the first time I was a victim of discrimination, yet I was surprised at what happened next. While the other classmates sat silent, Airman Rivera strongly challenged the professor. She explained everyone knew I had the highest average, so why wasn't I selected for the top award?

He looked perturbed and went on to explain what goes into the selection is more than academics alone; the whole person is considered. At this, Airman Rivera didn't miss a beat; she looked at him closely, sincerely, and said, "Well, what is wrong with Jones's whole person?"

This question was seared in my consciousness and arose at various points in my career. It was a valid question deserving an answer no one was willing to consider or give. Throughout the years, I would find myself longing for clarity to separate fact versus fiction concerning this 'whole person' theory. It seemed to me some people would always shift the rules to get the outcome of making me second, but I never let it stop me from striving.

I was stunned at how my feisty friend stood up to what we all deemed an injustice. The professor just got red in the face, raised his voice, and declared it was his classroom and it was just the way it was. She pushed back one last time and said defiantly that was not what he had told us when we'd begun the class. He would not budge, and while I was upset, I learned a valuable lesson concerning the unwritten rules and how easily the written 'rules' can be erased.

Therefore, on my graduation day in September 1997, I received a Distinguished Graduate certificate even though I had the highest academic average in the class.

It did not appear Sgt. Drexler valued my career or considered the impact of his decision on me; he merely wanted to ensure his choice student was set up for success. You may not be aware the Honor Graduate distinction sets an Airman apart upon arrival at their permanent duty station and aids them in future promotions.

This incident raised my resolve to continue being the best I could and to foster equity where I could. I knew prior to going for it that I would face unfair situations, but honestly, after listening to core values and how we were expected to conduct ourselves, this reeked of hypocrisy.

Upon leaving technical school, I was ready for my first duty assignment as a customer service clerk. It was the perfect position for me, and I enjoyed greeting customers and helping them resolve their issues. My previous position as a waitress made me a natural in this position. As a teenager, I had learned how to communicate properly and resolve customer complaints.

The military was the first place I'd found a sense of camaraderie in my adult life; it really was a family of sorts. There was never a time I could not find someone willing to assist me. As a young woman away from home for the first time, there were older female Airmen who mothered me and showed me the ropes. As I got older, young military women would ask me if it was possible to have a family and be in the military. They genuinely did not know; it was my honor to explain it was possible. It was also a clue I was getting old.

As a young girl, my grandparents both were interested in ensuring I had an idea of how to be of service to others. My grandmother would often tell me to treat everyone well because, as she put it, "you never know who you are going to need to ask to bring you a drink of water."

This has proved a valuable tip for me as I have embraced the shared humanity existing between us all. I truly do not believe I belong to any one group, but to all.

Last week, I was in an Uber in DC and my driver was from Haiti. He was delightful and as we chatted, he cautiously said to me, "You do not seem like you are American."

I said, "I don't? Where do I seem like I am from?" I thought he meant based on the way I looked, but he meant the way I behaved. I was used to not being considered fully American based on my skin. But he was expressing the way I went about being inclusive. He went on to explain I seemed very flexible and looked like I could be from anywhere. I took it as the compliment he intended it to be. What I heard him say was that I was a part of a larger society, and I love the sound and thought of transcending any one place.

My grandfather, Pop, made me keenly aware of this need in his own unique way. I have catalogued so many of the things he told me. He was a very funny man who could tell the greatest stories. I greatly valued the stories he shared with me.

One day, Pop was telling me about discrimination and said to me very bluntly, "There's always going to be a new nigger; sometimes it is you and sometimes it is someone else, so it's important you never treat anyone else poorly." He went on to explain throughout history, there has always been a group of people treated unfairly. The faces, races, and ethnicities change, but is no excuse to participate when your group is not impacted. I have always remembered his wisdom and as I watched the out-groups change in our society, his words rang true. If more people used this strategy, we would have less bullying and more tolerance, and certainly, we would have more people choosing service before self.

Excellence in All You Do

I spent twenty-one years, four months, and six days of my life in the United States military. It was an honor and a privilege to serve the nation's people. I count this as one of the best decisions I ever made. This one decision made at nineteen set me on a course and destination I could never have imagined for myself. Over the years, I found challenging assignments, had peers push me beyond my comfort zone, and felt stretched by leadership duties. During my military career, I served four years in the active duty Air Force and 17 years in the Air National Guard serving in the District of Columbia, Oklahoma, and Virginia Air National Guard. I loved being an Airmen.

Yet, in 2014, I decided to retire.

After the birth of my third child, I felt the urge to hang up my uniform. It was the end of an exciting era. No longer would my kids be able to wear t-shirts stating, "My mama wears combat boots," and I was fine with the new normal. It is funny, twenty years ago, the old timers, as we called them, were telling me, "You will know when it's time to go." This was some cryptic advice I never understood until it happened. One day, I just knew it was time and I have no regrets.

Early into my career, I developed a passion for equal opportunity issues, which eventually led to my assignment as an EEO officer. This was my favorite job in the military, as I saw it as an opportunity to tackle social justice issues from within an organization that touches the world. I can still vividly remember being interviewed for an officer position during my first pregnancy. I sat before an all-male interview board, in a maternity military uniform. The interview was going great until the final question. I could not believe one of the panel members asked me, "Who is going to take care of your baby if we select you and send you off to officer's school?"

I thought, *You have got to be kidding me.*

However, I replied as professionally as I could with humor, "Since this is the first grandchild on both sides of the family, both grandmothers can't wait to get their hands on my baby."

I walked out of the interview knowing I would not get the position. My prediction came true.

Miraculously, another military unit called me for an interview, and this time it was a female officer. I was so bummed by the first interview, I didn't anticipate a different outcome since I was further along in my pregnancy at this point. I was eight months pregnant and unable to drive to the interview, so they offered to conduct it on the phone. I then disclosed I could not drive the distance for an in-person second interview due to my doctor's orders.

To my astonishment, they waited until I delivered my baby to do a second-round face-to-face interview—and I was selected for commissioning.

Working in the Equal Opportunity Employment office exposed me to a new level of racial resilience. Not only did I need to adapt to racial adversity personally, but also, I assisted other people in their resilience journeys. Yet, when I went to interview for this position, I was asked a very interesting question. Before me sat two senior white male officers. Opening the interview was the following question, "Have you been discriminated against more because you are black or because you are a woman?"

I simply responded, "Since I am unable to separate the two, I have found people who don't respect one also do not respect the other."

They both perked up at my answer and explained they wanted me for the job.

After I was offered the position, the Colonel went on to explain he knew there were still parts of the States where the agency's diversity and inclusion message would be rejected. He also knew I as the messenger would not be accepted either—quite apart from how people took on the message I would deliver.

I was impressed with his honesty and his awareness; however, I wondered what he was doing to change this situation? The cultural climate he described was not surprising to me. I had been born and raised in Virginia and understood what I would be facing in trying to carry a message of equality. I faced an uphill battle with many key military leaders to understand the necessity for diversifying the agency.

On the surface, I had support, but there were several tense moments and memories I looked forward to forgetting.

This Air Force core value, I must say, was the one I saw the most in my military life, from others and myself. I purposely set out to do great work and be a person of excellence. I had a wonderful career filled with exciting projects, and nearly everyone I worked with was pursuing excellence. For the most part, it was a great work environment and I thrived at the idea of the newness every day brought. Most people join the military expecting adventure; I can assure you I found it there. If you are looking for adventure, consider the military as a viable option.

I have shared with you, at various points, how I was challenged with my running ability. However, one of the last challenges in my military officer's training required me to run three miles. I still laugh when I think about it, but being a person of excellence, I was determined to complete it. I practiced hard and knew I would not run it fast, but I wanted to complete it. I told my squad mates they would not win any team awards with me in tow, but I was going to finish it.

They understood and when they would see me running in the mornings, they would smile. I cannot overstate how slow of a runner I am.

When the day of the big run was upon me, I was nervous but prepared. I had run the whole month in preparation and my goal was completion, not time. At every mile, there was a check point with a medic, water, and those to encourage you. I ran my first mile and passed the check point, smiling; I wanted to run the entire time, not a run-walk like I had been doing in practice.

As I approached the second mile check point, I was jogging and nearly everyone had passed me, but trust me when I say I have no pride or ego concerning my running abilities.

As a matter of fact, the first military nickname given to me by my unit members was, "Lieutenant Turtle," after they watched me run. One of them asked me point blank, "Ma'am, are you running slow on purpose?"

Back to my final run, when I approached the check point, the medic asked, "Ma'am, are you ok, are you injured?"

I smiled and said, "I'm fine, I'm just a slow runner."

He looked at me and said, "Well, good job, keep it up."

I finished my three-mile run under forty-five minutes and I was so proud of myself. My teammates had long finished and even came back to run some of the last mile with me. I got a good laugh as I reflected on the look on the medic's face; he genuinely thought I was hurt.

It is the furthest distance I have run to date consecutively and I am still so proud of this accomplishment. This is one example of the purpose of intentional resilience; it is to complete the goals you set out to do. It is using the bootstraps to remind yourself you can do whatever you put your mind to doing, no matter how long it takes.

CHAPTER 4

THE BIBLE: THE PEACE OF SPIRITUAL RESILIENCE

"The Holy Scriptures are our letters from home."
Augustine of Hippo

"Live your life in such a way that others will come for miles to watch you burn."
John Wesley

I use the term "Bible" both literally and figuratively in this section. I am specifically addressing faith or belief in a higher power as a key element to overcoming adversity. What I am describing as spiritual resilience is any energy resource not manufactured by you individually.

You may equate it to a force lodged deep inside of you or outside of you, but it is not something you create or control. For those of you who are not believers in terms of religion or a prescribed faith, there is still much you can glean from using this type of resilience. Some will find this peace through meditation or deep reflection, and others through fasting, prayer, and incorporating scriptures into their memory and action plan. Others will draw on nature and the earth's beauty for inspiration and strength. I personally use all the above, because my personal faith is rested in one Creator who is responsible for mankind and assists everyone. This has brought me great peace in the darkest moments of life.

Stories have shaped cultures, nations, and societies. It is amazing to think how most of the ancestral history was passed through oral traditions and storytelling, long before we had a written language. Let us never lose our ability to connect in this manner. Its power is pertinent to encourage the next generation of service members and supporters. Through story, I wanted to paint a portrait of who I was, who I am, and who I am becoming.

Throughout history, we find stories of men and women who triumphed in unimaginable situations using spiritual techniques. This is a path I have walked on several occasions. I personally subscribe to a faith using the Bible as a source document and there is no way to share my truth or the ultimate source of my resilience without including it. It is my secret weapon and has sustained me when I wanted to give up.

If you do not share the same beliefs as I do, you can still gain insights from this section of the book. My spiritual belief system is the driving force for the totality of who and what I am and all I will ever become. It is the direct source of my inspiration, strength, and resilience. I make no apologies for it and do not try to hide it; it is as plain as the nose on my face. I have seen God's hand rescue me from literal and figurative burning buildings and I am fully convinced he will continue this work. Imagining God as a firefighter has been a source of calm for me because I know if He did it once, He can do it again.

I can overcome every situation, because I am convinced I have divine assistance and unlimited wisdom available. I am also positive I am never alone, even when I feel lonely or isolated from earthly people; this belief has increased my resilience tremendously.

There was a time when I operated in my own strength and relied on my natural grit.

This worked for a while, until I encountered an obstacle that was insurmountable in my human strength. We will all face these at some point in our lives and learn valuable lessons from them.

Faith has proven to be a critical component making the most impossible situations bearable. We all place our faith in something, whether we are aware of it or not. In the past, I have placed faith and trust in people, which led to great disappointment. I have learned, through trials, to place my trust in God because He does not disappoint.

I have also gained a great deal of understanding of how to overcome adversity from the lives of the women and men in the Bible. There are great pearls of knowledge one can glean from the steps taken by inspiring characters, heroes, and legends.

Often, I conceptualize one's spiritual foundation as the foundation of a house. The biblical foundation I was provided is built to sustain hurricane winds and hazardous weather. It may be a good time to stop and think about how you conceptualize *your* foundation.

When everything falls apart and you find yourself standing in a pile of rubble, is there concrete or sand beneath your feet? You will want to access this before the big one strikes.

Often, faith is credited with what sustained African slaves and their descendants in America. This has been researched, documented, and passed on as a legacy to encourage future generations. The Black Church and Black people in general have historically been deemed resilient.

Watching the images of the Civil Rights era confirmed this belief internationally. Pulling on an inner strength given by a higher power has been historically acknowledged and passed on. I was certainly taught this at an early age and have taught my children to pursue the peace that comes from trusting in the spiritual nature of God.

Dare I speak about the mysterious components man has yet to fully theorize, conceptualize, or thoroughly explain? I am passionate about this type of resilience, because it saved my life and is directly responsible for my ability to move forward when my feet were deep in concrete and mud. My perspective is unpolluted by the impact uncertainty once held in my life and I firmly believe the future is full of good things and possibilities waiting for you and me.

Looking at the conditions Blacks endured through a lens of spiritual resilience helps to frame a portrait of perseverance, determination, and hope.

It's a portrait painted by several ethnic groups throughout history.

American-Indians held on to this hope as well while they walked the Trail of Tears. They were known as a people with no past or future due to significant losses during the forced migration to the west in the mid-1800's, yet even as they walked, they did so with a spiritual force guiding their footsteps and speaking into their future. Along the path known as the Trail of Tears is a flower known as the Cherokee Rose. It is said that those who walked the path believed it was a sign from the

Creator acknowledging their sorrow and tears. It is ironic to note that slaves of African ancestry walked the Trail of Tears also and suffered loss. This confirms what I have shared with others for years, which is that "No one owns suffering." No one group of people can stake a claim to own tragedy and loss, because we as humans have a history of unimaginable sorrow.

Holocaust survivors are another group who leveraged spiritual resilience.

Nelson Mandela is also known to credit his spiritual belief with being able to endure what were unimaginable conditions in South Africa. My point is you can look at any historical tragedy and find people who pursued peace through spiritual practices.

I am one of those people and I credit the biblical scriptures with providing a clue to how to deal with adversity, which is found in Revelation 12:11, "And they overcome him by the blood of the Lamb and by the word of their testimony."

I have committed this scripture to my memory and my frequent practice; I encourage you to consider doing the same. It will remind you how important it is to tell others your adversity stories and how vital it is to point them in God's direction.

In the Beginning

"The Bible is the cradle in which Christ was laid."
Martin Luther

At an early age, my grandmothers introduced me to the concept of God. He was a real person included in decision-making and daily life, and He was necessary in times of trouble.

His unseen hand was responsible for the food on the table and any good coming into our home in the form of blessings. As a young child, I attended church on most Sundays with my Big Mama, Vacation Bible School in the summer, revival services, and the early morning Easter service.

I sang in the children's choir and my first memory of this includes the image of wanting to make my great grandfather proud. I worked hard to remember the words and smiled big as I sang. Church was a place for family, faith, and fun in my childhood and I have attempted to duplicate this for my children as well.

As I got older, Big Mama started applying a bit of pressure for me to be baptized. To her, the ticket to heaven was water baptism, but I was not ready. My grandfather (Pop) pulled me to the side privately and explained that when I was ready, I would know. The way he explained it was I would know when I was ready because I would feel God tugging at my heart.

He also told me there was no magic in the baptismal pool water; in his life, he had seen many people go down in the water as dry devils, only to come out of the water as wet devils.

We would laugh and laugh, but only if we were out of my Big Mama's earshot. This was no laughing matter because she believed part of her responsibility was to ensure her family would remain intact in Heaven after this life ended. Therefore, all through my teenage years, this became a burden for her since none of her grandchildren was baptized.

As I got older, I attended church less frequently due to moving farther away from my grandmother. I just never felt the tug at my heart; however, I knew an unseen force was working in my life. This was undeniable, I would often think back to my earliest memories of God and wonder if it was Him I could sense.

When I was fifteen, I met my future husband and started attending church with his family. They went to church every Sunday without fail and I found myself back in the presence of the God I had sung about as a little girl. I was mostly an observer and often read the book of Revelations during the service. I could not begin to tell you what any sermon was about; I only listened to the songs and the announcements. The rest of my time, I found myself flipping through the pages of the Bible and ultimately reading the most difficult book within it. I never knew why I was drawn to the section, but Sunday after Sunday, it was what I was reading.

Honestly, I went because I wanted to spend time with my boyfriend, but I found myself involved in the choir, the church plays, and becoming a part of the church community. I was fascinated with the way in which people genuinely seemed connected with their faith and belief. I was also intrigued and entertained by my boyfriend's mother who had no shame in praising God. She would lift her hands, cry, and shout, "Hallelujah" or "Amen." I would often think to myself, "What is wrong with that woman?"

When I asked my boyfriend, he remarked, "She really loves God."

It seemed strange to me, because I had only witnessed this once before in my Big Mama's church. When I was very little, I remember there was a very old man seated in the corner of the church. He began humming, and singing, and crying, and then shouting something about how good God was. Men began to rush over to him ensuring he did not fall and to calm him down. It was a strange occurrence, because our church was very scripted in those days and his outburst was odd.

I was terrified and did not know what was happening; it was quite the scene in our little, calm church. My eyes were as big as a quarter and I stood trying to see what was happening. Big Mama squeezed my hand, and I sat down with tears in my eyes, because I thought he may have been sick. I asked her what happened to him, and she gently replied the spirit of God had touched him.

I had no idea what it meant but was worried at the thought God may touch me and make me act like that in public too. Well, there I was watching my future mother-in-law ten years later being touched by God and she was acting just like the old man I remembered.

My faith walk began in my mind and was characterized by the seeds planted in my childhood. Many people I met along the way nurtured it; however, in 1993, this faith shifted from my mind into my heart and was the beginning of an incredible transition. It was the moment my Big Mama had waited and prayed for, the day I felt the Lord tugging at my heart as my Pop had described, and the day I answered, "Yes."

I was in basic training and it was a low point for me personally. I was miserable and the only escape from the misery was the few hours of retreat one could find at Chapel services on Sunday. It was the only place you were safe from the wrath of drill instructors. Every trainee had to cope with the pressures, and we all did it differently. There were those of us who were obviously stressed and a few girls who were unnerved by the daily drama.

One day, I asked my friend Loraine how she remained so calm and I was shocked to hear her answer. She told me early in the morning, before anyone else was awake, she would sneak into the day room and read her Bible. Reading the good book was the first thing she did and praying at night was the last thing she did. She said God helped her get through the day.

She then turned to me and said, "You should try it." I was a little embarrassed, because we were the same age and yet she seemed years ahead of me in wisdom. Since I always struggled with getting up at 5 a.m., I knew I would never be able to do what she did, but I began to look for other ways to incorporate God into my day and my life.

My life has been filled with amazing people who have pointed me in the right direction when I was off course and Loraine is one example of this. She challenged me to look for something outside of myself to help me with what was a most difficult set of circumstances. Shortly, after our encounter, she suffered an injury causing her to be transferred to another flight, but I met her months later and thanked her for her insight and direction. Her recommendation concerning faith changed my life for the better.

It has been reported, "There are no atheists in foxholes." I would like to tell you, "There are no atheists in basic training either." Whether you believed in God or not, everyone went to church for respite and the ability to be free for a few hours. Guys went to church to spend time with the girls and vice versa. I found myself faithfully at church and it is where I felt the need to surrender my life to Jesus Christ.

At a church far from home on Lackland AFB, I felt God touch my heart in a way I could not ignore. The day of my baptism was serene. There were two of us taking a life-changing step, and while I don't remember the gentleman's name, we are bound together forever as brother and sister in Christ. It was a special occasion and one of the few happy memories I have from basic training. I promptly mailed the certificate home to my Big Mama. When she died twelve years later, the certificate was in the stack of her special papers.

Obedience is Better than Sacrifice

"Don't fall into the trap of studying the Bible without doing what it says."

Francis Chan

This saying was one of my grandmother's go-to phrases when she wanted to articulate the need to do what the Bible said. She was a firm believer we should not tempt God. When she said it, what she meant was you do not want to find out what happens when you don't do things God's way.

I find myself repeating this phrase often also.

It is amazing how quickly we turn into our parents and grandparents. Long before I really knew what it meant, I was quoting it to others. I used it to keep myself on what I considered a straight and narrow path. It was effective and served as a guide for right living.

The early days of my military career presented me with significant challenges I had never faced before. It was really the first time in my life I felt weak and afraid. I had gotten myself into a situation I could not control. But in the middle of the situation, I became intrigued by the spiritual resilience I saw in two of my classmates. One was a girl from Nebraska; she was the biggest, strongest, and sweetest in our flight. She was very nice and never caused any trouble.

Every night, they would call lights out at 9 p.m. Her bunk was close to mine, so when lights went out, I would see her using a small flashlight under her sheet to read her Bible.

I knew this and would watch and wonder what was so interesting. I had read some of the Bible while sitting in church back home, but never picked one up to read just for the fun of it, like she did. But she was disciplined, and this was her nightly routine.

Every flight has an Airman who holds the position of dorm chief. This is a member of the flight who serves as an internal leader to ensure the rules are being followed. Our dorm chief who happened to be the oldest member of the flight and a mother came around ensuring we were all in our bunks for the night. She noticed Airman Boyd was reading under her covers and told her to cut the light out. Airman Boyd said she would be done in a few minutes very politely. The dorm chief was abrupt and liked being in power, so she rudely told her to cut the light off now, because it was lights out. Some of us started saying things like "leave her alone," "she never bothers anybody," and "she's not bothering us."

The dorm chief became incensed and walked over closer to make her point.

Airman Boyd, who—remember—was the strongest and biggest, got up and, in a very loud voice, said, "I am reading my Bible, and I will read my Bible and no one in here is going to stop me from reading my Bible. Do you understand? I must read my Bible." By then, she was crying and trembling, and the dorm chief was scared. We had never seen this girl raise her voice or have any emotional reaction, but I can tell you this: she read her Bible every night from then on with no interruptions.

I thought somehow maybe her grandmother had taught her the one prevailing scripture I heard growing up in the form of "obedience is better than sacrifice." My grandmother loved quoting this as much as many of the things older folks instilled in me; I did not understand it until I had a few years under my belt. By then, I had quoted it so much it had meaning beyond what she originally meant. This young woman was a visual display of obedience; despite the cost or consequences, she was going to read her Bible daily. Even though I did not exactly understand the fervency with which she approached this, all of us, believers or non-believers, respected it. We admired her desire to take a stand for what she believed in, and after all these years, I often think of her and how she will never know how her tenacity inspired me.

After basic training, everyone went in separate directions and I was given orders to work in Missouri. Being from Virginia, I was not used to the Midwest winters. When I arrived, the first thing I needed was a car. I could barely afford one, but I went to the dealership and bought the only car I could afford. It was a Mazda GLC, and when the salesman asked me if I knew what it stood for, I shook my head no, and he said, "Good little car."

He was correct; the car was great even though I did not know how to drive a stick. One of my co-workers went with me to pick up the car and he took me to the fairground afterwards, where he taught me how to drive the stick in a couple of hours.

The following week, a major snowstorm rolled into the area. I woke up and looked out the window; there was snow everywhere with a thick blanket covering the car, so I went back to sleep. Thirty minutes later, the phone rang in the dorm, and when I answered it, it was my boss.

He said, "Where are you?"

I replied, "I'm at the dorm."

There was a slight pause and then he said, "Aren't you supposed to be at work?"

I was surprised and I said, "But, it's snowing."

He was patient and finally said, "Where are you from?"

I said, "Virginia."

He laughed and said, "You are in Missouri now and you are still expected to report to work when it snows."

I said "yes, sir" and got dressed as quick as I could and slid all the way into work, while driving the good little car.

When I arrived, my boss was shaking his head and laughing. I was embarrassed as he told some of the other team members. I really did not know, as no one briefed me on the winter protocol. I told him everything shuts down in Virginia when it snows. He understood, but I tell you, it was a hard winter on me. My body was used to looking at snow as a day to sleep in, and in Missouri, it was a day to get up early to dig yourself out.

All was not lost though; I learned to drive a stick *and* to drive in snow.

One of my fellow Airmen was a young woman from Jamaica who was quite interesting. She taught me a lot about being true to one's faith. She was hilarious and the first person I knew who would fast for religious purposes. Fasting is the process of not eating for a certain time period. Many people pray instead of eating during this period. From time to time, she would look very mean and I would ask her what was bothering her. Then she would look at me and say, "I am fasting for my attitude."

I would giggle and say, "Good."

She too confirmed for me what my grandmother taught me. Her obedience to fasting was better than the sacrifice of what her unchecked attitude could have cost her. Her example and her dedication to her faith also provided an example to follow. She was a no-nonsense, hard worker. I was fortunate to have had wonderful young women placed in my life at the right time.

"This Too Shall Pass"

"I've read the last page of the Bible; it's all going to turn out alright."

Billy Graham

When I was growing up, one of the most frequently quoted scriptures was, "This too shall pass." At the time, I did not know it was from the Bible, but my great aunt would quote it for nearly everything. She was a no-nonsense type of woman who frequently had a serious look on her face. She was one of the elders for whom you made sure you were on your best behavior.

Whenever the kids would have disagreements or complaints arose to her level, she would simply remark, "This too shall pass."

What does that mean to a seven-year-old?

It was a very cynical remark to make to a young child, yet I credit her words and the lesson she taught me. When I reached adulthood, I credited her words and temperament with preparing me for adversity. Whenever I faced trials, I knew they would not last forever due to this scripture taught to me as a child, and this gave me confidence and hope. Her demeanor was never alarmed despite us rushing in the house in a panic or our anxiety. Unnerved by our childish dilemmas, she rarely looked up from the paper she was reading as she responded with her favorite verse.

I often found my great aunt unpleasant to be around, due to her sometime callous nature and smug responses. I detested the tone of her voice when she was correcting me and then there was a word she loved to use. The word was "vulgar"; she loved to use it as a rebuke or a warning about how she perceived what I said or did. Once again, I had no idea what the word meant, but by the way it rolled off her lips, I perceived it to be a dirty word and a jab at me.

One day, I summoned the courage to ask my grandmother why she was so mean. Growing up, I did not think she liked me, and as a young child, this belief was difficult because I prided myself on everyone liking me. The only person who could really make her smile was my grandpa and she knew how much he loved me, so I assumed she would love me also. My grandmother told me she lost her son in a tragic car accident and explained how the loss changed her. She helped me to see it was not anything personal about me, but her heart had been broken from the loss of her son. Knowing her truth shifted the way I interacted with her and loved her going forward.

I share this with you to encourage you to empathize with others when their behaviors toward you do not make sense. It is also a great example of not shying away from the more difficult personalities in your life, because they may provide you with something that could help you later. I learned such valuable lessons from her and began to see her differently. I wanted to give her extra hugs when I saw her, and she has the honor of permanently searing a Bible verse into my memory. Essentially, she put a tattoo on my soul which has never faded away.

Several years ago, I was provided this same proverb in a different way by an Army Colonel. I was serving on a joint tour with the Army and he was my direct supervisor. He was a very interesting character who was the calmest person I think I've ever met. One day, I called him in a panic. There was major chaos in my section, and I felt threatened by a superior officer in a meeting. It always took a lot to get me rattled and I was very upset about what was happening. As I spoke fast and in a high-pitched voice, I am sure the Colonel was silent. He let me speak, and finally he called my name to stop me from talking. The second time he said it, I stopped. He then said in a very assertive manner, "Captain Allen, you're a big girl."

That stopped me dead in my tracks, and in a second, I was reminded who I was.

He proceeded to say, "You do not get worried until I get worried. Do I seem worried to you?"

"No, sir," I responded. I hung up the phone with a renewed optimism.

The fear and uncertainty plaguing me then was such a short reality. What I was worried about never manifested and the people seeking to alter my future did not have the power or chance. My Colonel forced me to draw upon my spiritual resilience with his assertion that I was a big girl. When he said it, something inside of me agreed with his words. I was neither small nor helpless. I was a big girl, who had a big God on her side, and for this reason, I did not have to fear what seemed like giants approaching. It was a timely reminder, and now when I face difficulty, I often think to myself, "You are a big girl," which often causes me to laugh.

For most of my life, I have sought to control situations before they happened through strategic planning. This worked until I realized I was not in charge of the universe or myself. Really, there is very little I am in direct control of, and if I had learned this lesson earlier, I could have saved myself a great deal of stress. I can vividly remember sitting at my desk when I was pregnant with my son, calculating how old I would be at his high school graduation, when I would retire, and calculating his college graduation.

I was a controller and did not realize how disruptive this was to my faith. How could God implement His plans for me, when I was busying ensuring my calculations were enforced?

It is amazing how long this went on and how patient God must have been. I imagine Him watching me all these years must have provided regular programming for a Comedy Central show in Heaven. I can see Jesus laughing now saying, "There she goes again; when will she ever learn?"

I got the message loud and clear on several occasions, but I must be a slow learner because it took a major disappointment for me to understand God was in control.

I had to take my hands off the wheel and let Him drive.

I wish I could tell you I willingly gave control of the wheel over to Him, but it would be untrue. Despite the circumstances, He got the wheel, and I am uninterested in taking it back these days. I like riding in the passenger seat, as there are so many things I now see I have missed all those years. I fully understand the essence of the tattoo I bear from my great aunt; I know the peace that comes with knowing my current situation is temporary and will eventually pass.

It is reassuring to look back on my past struggles and realize I am no longer burdened by them. Even if the people who hurt me are still a part of my life, the pain is not nearly intense as it was in the moment. It has passed, and I say to you with all I believe in it does pass. When the next overwhelming wave of life hits, just stare it straight in the eye and declare, "This too shall pass."

And the Greatest of These is Love

"Most people are bothered by those passages of Scripture they do not understand, but the passages that bother me are those I do understand."

Mark Twain

Love is a required concept in the Christian faith and is supposed to be a visible sign and beacon to the world. It is one way we validate that we are who we say we are. One of the most valuable and difficult leadership lessons to date, for me, was to love people who did not love me back. Most of my career, I found myself in a wide variety of military settings. I was successful, well-liked, and a hard worker. This served me well, and eventually I took on higher-level leadership positions and accepted one in which I was part of the executive management team.

I was excited, nervous, but mostly eager to lead my team into victory. Some of the team members did not accept my vision or leadership. Up until this point, I had been very successful and had not tasted failure or rejection, making this a difficult season.

I learned many valuable lessons from this leadership trial, but the greatest of these lessons was love. There were many humbling days on this job. I had never worked anywhere where I was not celebrated, and was in for a rude awakening in my new environment where I was barely tolerated by some of the employees. There were red flag warnings I refused to heed, because I wanted the opportunity. There's a carefully placed warning in scripture I failed to consider. It says, "Pride goeth before the fall," and in many ways, this assignment felt like flying down a set of steep steps. When I first reported for my preliminary in-processing, the head of security was sizing me up. She was a no-nonsense gal and she pointblank looked at me and said, "I think you are too nice for this job." She was serious and I just laughed it off.

I spent quite a few hours over the next few years in her office seeking solace in my best attempt to learn the culture and the resistance of the people. She would often remind me she had tried to warn me, and we would both laugh. Those moments of comic relief provided me an outlet in lieu of the river of tears churning on the inside of me.

One day, I got my biggest laugh ever, when she told me that some people believed I had HR magic and had somehow used my human resources powers to blind the senior leaders. They believed this was the reason I had not been fired. It could not have been possible I was competent, and they were wrong, of course; therefore, I must have been some type of witch.

I laughed for months at the assertion and realized there was no reasoning or negotiating with people who refused to accept my leadership or knowledge. It wasn't funny, but once again I was masking my pain with humor. To think that if I had magical powers, I would use them in the office instead of on the lottery is ludicrous!

This was what I called my first leadership failure and I took it very hard. Yet, I learned the most valuable lessons in this position. The lesson prepared me for what came next. Failure is a part of the learning process; it is rarely enjoyable, but an effective instructor. Learning to love people despite their actions has opened an entirely new world for me and allowed me to be authentic. For far too long, I was a people pleaser and realized it was a waste of energy and time. Some people will never accept you or respect you, but this cannot be a stop sign, because it is nothing more than a bend in the road.

Once I accepted this truth, it changed my thinking even though it never changed my environment. I did not leave the position until I had mastered the lessons God wanted to teach me.

It kept me on my toes and on my knees. There were many days I shut my door and cried. Yet, in those trying times, I prayed for my staff, my enemies, and my leaders. I was taught a valuable lesson concerning the necessity of using love as a buffer to combat hatred. It was inconceivable to me that so many people did not appreciate my easygoing, fun-loving approach to life.

I smiled all the time and spoke to everyone I met, even when they did not speak back.

This was a moment of maturity for me; I had reached the level of leadership that made it hard for people to separate my title and position from my individuality. I was not human in some people's eyes; I was the institution or, even worse, I was "The man."

Happiness has always been my baseline emotion; however, I have realized some people don't like it when others are very happy. I am always smiling even in the worst of situations; it is my natural tendency. It is almost a trademark for me. I am known to always smile, but it was hard for me to understand when a co-worker genuinely did not like me. As a peacemaker, I am the first to attempt resolution. I am normally very successful in this area, yet I have had a few unfortunate occasions when my happy disposition was not appreciated. In one incident, I ended up in my supervisor's office listening to a co-worker attempt to explain the issues she had with me.

I was really hoping for a happy ending, because I never knew what had soured her against me. Not only was she difficult to work with, but she was also disrespectful to me publicly. I was cautious in how to handle this because I did not want to be labeled the angry black woman. Once applied, this stereotype can be very difficult to erase. It is seen as the kiss of death in the black community and I had fought against this label my entire career.

My supervisor was tired of hearing her complain about me, and since she refused to communicate directly with me, he thought it wise to bring us together. My supervisor and I were both baffled during this conversation because this woman could name no legitimate concerns except the fact that she just did not like me. She had heard what people were saying about me and no longer liked me. However, she was not brave enough to state the truth in the meeting; the truth was to reveal the racially charged accusations that continued to swirl around me from the first to the last day I worked there. Employees watched who visited my office or who I was seen talking to in the halls for demographic trends. Then, they would launch complaints with the data.

My supervisor desperately wanted this situation to go away and remarked to me when she left the office that I needed to fix this. Once again, how did I fix my leading while being black which seemed to drive some people crazy?

I made it very clear to him that I did not need the woman to like me, but to act professionally. I also reminded him that he was her supervisor and that was his responsibility not mine.

I was uncomfortable by what appeared to be two grown women looking foolish over such trivial issues. It irked me when male leaders were quick to call two females in to resolve issues but allowed the male employees to fight amongst themselves. I was disgusted at the fact that years of hard work and achievements had landed me in the position of looking like a schoolgirl not getting along with another girl in the playground. The gender dynamics did not escape me in this meeting and left a bitter taste in my mouth. I wondered, didn't this woman know she was setting us back with her refusal to resolve her issues with me privately? I did not have a smile on my face, and I realized once again my brown skin was wreaking havoc.

This was, unfortunately, confirmed and noted as being the culprit by several internal and external employees. What was I to do with the assertion that I was going to be judged harsher or watched more closely by employees because I was chocolate ice cream instead of vanilla-flavored?

I had to love them, and I chose to forgive them, as they were missing out on the best I had to offer the world because of the wrapper. My only choice was to press on, to see what I could garner from the situation to make me better.

I chose to look closely at the criticisms of my critics and search for any truth.

I asked my closest staff if they saw any racial disparity in my treatment of employees and I became a student of my behavior. Everyone has blind spots and it is important to ask for others to help you. I found, at the end of the day, there were always going to be people who would look at me and want me to go back to Africa. My chosen response was to continue to try to understand their perspective when appropriate, and to love them. It is still my response.

I do all this while ensuring they know I am just as much an American as they are, and at this time, I don't have any blood relatives or land in Africa that I am aware of.

I know their rationale is justified by them and their reasoning is more complicated and complex, but the point is I have stood and continue to stand at the intersection of race and resilience, wondering if I need to build a permanent home here or a hostel I frequent from time to time. I realize race will always be a part of my adversity journey, but I believe I have transcended some of the polarizing moments of my past and learned to better navigate this world in my beautiful, brown skin. I have used love to teach others how to embrace inclusion and how to love themselves.

I want to end this section with a call for self-love.

Self-love is a requirement if you are to maintain resilience. There will be moments when you must look yourself in the face and remember what makes you uniquely you and what makes you great. I had to remind myself of this on more than one occasion when the voices of the naysayers were shouting insults at me.

Bouncing Back vs. Bouncing Back Better

I imagine many of you are more than likely attempting to prepare for adversity or suffering from the effects of it and are in search of some practical steps. I am writing this section just for you.

I do not take it lightly that you have gotten to this point in the book and consider it an honor that you're seeking assistance and answers.

I want to provide some thoughts concerning this, using the acronym "FURNITURE."

Resilience has served as a classic piece of furniture in my metaphorical home. Sometimes, it was a comfy chair, and other times, served as a sturdy table. My goal is to bounce back better from every situation I face going forward.

You will find the comparison in this table:

Bouncing Back	Bouncing Back Better
Focused on your problem	Focused on your future
Using your strength	Using your spirit
Ready for a change	Ready for a transition
Needs support system	Needs to become a support system to someone else
Interprets the current state as the ideal	Interprets the current state as today, not tomorrow
Transactional	Transformational
Uncertainty causes fear	Uncertainty causes fervor
Renewal	Revival
Establishing old territories	Establishing new territories

©2019, Antoinette Allen

Bouncing back is an initial goal; it is not the end goal. You have a unique opportunity to create a new way of being after experiencing adversity. After deep reflection, you may find new insights and emotional connections to explore. This exploration could lead you to a new way of operating or organizing your life. Do not be in such a hurry; you may miss a growth opportunity.

There are some things I have lived through which yielded great insights, solidifying my resilience, but of course, I will not voluntarily explore them again.

Oftentimes, during the resilience process, I imagine myself as a bouncing ball that continued to bounce longer than I would have liked, yet the extra bounces made me better and allowed me to travel to distances and places I would not have gone if the bouncing stopped earlier.

I am in favor of bouncing back quickly, but have forced this on myself in times when it would have been prudent to slow the process down.

When you make your bed, you are going to lie in it

The above heading is one of the most overused colloquialisms given to me as a warning when I was growing up. Everyone in my family would share it as a well-established fact.

I have found it to be true also, but I want to put a positive spin on it. I want to use it as a quick reminder for you of what you can do when you find yourself in a difficult place you don't want to be, whether you caused the trouble or not.

One day, you may wake up and discover yourself lying in a bed of sadness, pain, oppression, or turmoil. Whatever the bed is, you can use the following resilience steps to change the sheets, so to speak. These steps will move you from the bed to the floor, and where you go from there is entirely up to you.

Stand Up (Be Curious)

This is the best time to reflect upon what led up to this event in the first place.

Examine your life through the eyes of an investigator. Years ago, I worked for a law enforcement agency and had firsthand insight into the strategies and minds of investigators. In the military, I conducted investigations as well, but this skill was often underutilized when it came time to assess my life and the choices leading up to some of the beds I was often lying in.

Instead of lamenting life's unexpected twists and turns, grow curious about them. Assign yourself as the lead investigator into this case and determine what good can be gleaned from it. Get curious about: the who, what, when, where, and how; the why may never be discovered, so do not bother making it the focus. Look at yourself with an outsider's eye, taking the time to re-discover who you are.

Once you become curious about who you are, you will find an excitement about who you are becoming. Take the posture of curiosity, and an energy that will begin to fill you, and before long, it will propel you out of the bed of affliction.

You will be back standing up firmly on your feet in no time. Life has a way of knocking all of us down at times, but curiosity is like a balloon lifting us into the air.

This was true for me during the most difficult times in my life. *Devastation* would be putting it mildly as an accurate depiction of what I experienced when a former supervisor informed me some of my leadership challenges were because of my skin color.

He told me my situation in the office would not likely improve until several people retired. In an instant, I was a teenager again being told that I must be in the wrong place, only this time it wasn't a church, it was an organization. There were few instances in my adult life where I felt uncomfortable in my own skin, but I experienced it every day I walked down the hall in this job.

It was a disappointing meeting and I left feeling defeated. I was prepared to hear about my weaknesses, because I was ready to work to remedy them. I was very confused by what I was hearing, since I was black when I was interviewed, black when I was hired and black when I first reported to work. I looked at him and jokingly said, "You do know this skin color does not wash off at night?" Every moment of every day after the meeting, it was on my mind and every decision I made was filtered through a racial lens. I had to check an extra box trying to ensure my actions weren't misinterpreted, but more often than not, they were.

I have never viewed my skin color as a weakness that should be overcome.

I did find a need to navigate the leadership waters differently since there were few black swimmers in the organizational waters. When I got home that night, I found myself lying on my bed, with my mind spinning, my heart broken, and my soul shaken. As I lay in the bed, blaming myself and relishing the fact I had to lie there, something amazing happened.

I heard deep in my spirit, "Get up from the bed of affliction."

I did not have the strength, will, or know-how, but I was receiving a demand, not a request. I physically got out of the bed and stood up, because I realized I could not lie there forever.

I firmly believe it was the voice of the Creator, the One who shaped me with His hands and His heart. I imagine His plan for my life could not be executed from my bed of affliction, so the order was sent for me to get up. I decided to get up because I knew I had people depending on me. How would I tell my children I was throwing in the towel? I was busy preparing them for life and teaching them how to be strong—so how could I lie there and be weak?

In my moments of weakness, I knew I was expected to get up, I could get up, and I was being told to get up. While it was a logical next step, it was not easy.

Once my feet were on the ground, I got very curious about my life, my situation, and my way forward. I would not be stopped by bias, cultural insensitivities, or the extra melanin which gave me a brown skin color. I would do the job I was hired to do to the best of my ability until it was time to move on. I would ignore the naysayers and see through the veiled racism and hold my head high, knowing I was fearfully and wonderfully made. No one else can do this for you; you should be curious about yourself. Bras will support your curiosity, but only you can light this spark.

Step Back, then Step Down (Endure)

"You therefore must endure hardship as a good soldier of Jesus Christ. No one engaged in warfare entangles himself with the affairs of this life, that he may please him who enlisted him as a soldier."

2 Timothy 2:3-4.

While I am an optimist, I am also a realist and I understand there are circumstances and situations that do not resolve quickly or quietly. Endurance will serve you well as a resilience step.

You may as well set your mind to the endurance dial, because you may not have a choice in the matter anyway. You will face untimely interruptions you cannot control. Get used to them and learn to expect them.

I remember standing in an emergency room on Christmas Day, broken from the realization I was having a third miscarriage. I was numb and nearly inconsolable, yet there in the emergency room was a woman who shifted my perspective.

I had known all the warning signs, so I was not surprised my body was betraying me again; I was saddened at the loss. I did not want to leave my oldest daughter who was diligently playing with her toys. I wanted a Christmas miracle, but it did not come in the manner I was hoping for.

When I arrived at the ER, I was in pain physically and emotionally. The greatest of these were the waves of anger taking me under yet again. I was being sucked into the undertow of unfulfilled dreams and visions of motherhood. I was drowning in my sorrow and barely staying afloat by hanging on to a thread of hope. Maybe, somehow, this pregnancy would be viable despite the obvious signs my body was sending.

I stood at the hospital reception desk waiting to be seen; the woman standing in front of me was drunk and appeared disheveled. The nose of a bloodhound and the smell of alcohol were making me nauseous. I would love to say I did not judge this woman, but the truth is I did. When she turned around and caught a glimpse of me, she stepped aside and told the receptionist to take me first. I was bent over, but I think I whispered, "Thank you."

Little did I know she was going to teach me a valuable lesson about endurance.

A few hours later, I ran into her in the hallway on my way to the restroom. When I passed by her, she looked at me and I began to weep. I just could not hold onto the pain anymore; I could no longer pretend to be strong in front of my husband and something about seeing another woman compelled me to be vulnerable. A great sense of shame was plaguing me in addition to the sadness. This woman wrapped her arms around me and held me as if I was a baby, while I wept. No words were necessary; somehow, she understood. I was very uncomfortable with this lack of control, but there I was standing in the hallway of a hospital being consoled by a woman whose clothes were dirty and who reeked of alcohol. None of it mattered; the universal language of love transcended our racial, socio-economic conditions, and my inherent distaste for the smell of alcohol.

When I was able to pull myself together, she explained to me when she was standing at the front desk, she turned around and looked into my eyes. She said she instantly recognized the pain on my face. She shared that she suffered from lupus, and that her body attacked every fetus she conceived, and she had suffered numerous miscarriages. Since diagnosis, she had never been able to have a child, so when she looked in my eyes, she saw a reflection of her pain.

This shifted my perspective. Yes, I was experiencing significant loss, but I had a beautiful daughter at home I could be thankful for. My disappointment had clouded my ability to focus more on what I had, versus what I did not have.

While she was consoling me, my husband was chatting with her boyfriend and discovered they were sleeping in their car. He said they were headed to the emergency room on the west side of town, when they felt a strong urge to turn around and go to the east side of town. They thought this was weird, but they both felt the urge and agreed to do it even though they were afraid they would run out of gas. They both agreed and there we all stood in the right place at the right time to bless each other. My husband, who has a heart for the homeless, gave them some assistance and decreed it as a Christmas miracle.

Her ability to endure the chronic loss in her life was an inspiration to me, and when I suffered my fourth and final miscarriage, I was able to grieve the loss appropriately. This time, I extended myself grace and let go of the shame and anger causing me to stay flat on my back in a bed of affliction.

Endurance has a two-step resilience process. This is due to the extended time many of us spend reflecting when bouncing back. The word "endure" denotes it is not a fast-moving concept, and thus we should not expect to yield the most benefits from a rushed process. This realization is often frustrating, especially for people like me who like to be in control of timelines. I learned the hard way to let those aspirations go.

Despite my best efforts, the universe refused to take orders or suggestions from me. It continued to move at its own pace and I chose to endure it. Accepting this is what allows the third resilience step to emerge. Once you realize you are a part of something bigger and greater than yourself, you will have to effectively put your foot forward to step down.

Stepping down is often where we give up the keys to our private kingdom and join the rest of the world. We see there are already established kingdoms we were meant to be a part of and we seek to make our home among them. We begin to realize we have something to offer and leverage our courage, curiosity, and humility to take the necessary steps.

Step three makes us brave; many people stop at this step and think this return to the normal world is the best they can hope for, but it is not. There is one final step which, when taken, will propel you to heights you never imagined possible before the setback.

Stand Up   Step Down   Step Back   Stand Out

©2019, Antoinette Allen

Stand Out (Don't Lose Heart)

Think of the woman who held me in the hospital; she was well-versed with the concept of endurance. Her divinely orchestrated meeting with me propelled her into a visible showing of the final resilience step. Regardless of the heartbreak and suffering this woman intimately knew, she still had a measure of love to pour out to a stranger.

She did not lose her humanity or heart in the process of pain. This, in turn, caused her to stand out; she has a place in my memory and my heart. "Do Not Lose Heart" is the tattoo of the resilient; it shouts in the face of adversity, "I am not giving up."

Why do some people fall apart and never get back up, while others rise stronger?

Why is some people's resilience the equivalent of the fictional character Rocky Balboa? This is a complicated question and numerous factors come into play. I encourage you to look at the details of your life for clues concerning your current resilience. Do you lose heart easily? Do you stand out? When I was a teenager, my mother told me, "Do not wear your heart on your sleeve, because if you do, anybody will be able to knock it off." I did not know what she meant, but she explained I was allowing too many people to affect my emotions. She helped me to know it was my responsibility to manage my emotions and to expect emotional bruises as a part of life.

Step one can be the hardest when our goal is to bounce back better. Often, it requires great personal courage and even sacrifice, yet it is so worth it. Letting go of how you thought your life was going to be can be frightening and unnerving. This is where courage comes into the picture; it is not the absence of fear but doing something despite the fear. It is when you stand up that you will begin to conceptualize new possibilities. No matter how comfortable you currently are, you need to get up because you cannot hide under the covers another day.

Step two may be easier after you have the momentum of standing, but it is a two-step process.

I suggest you step down before you step back. Metaphorically, I consider stepping down as the implementation of humility. I include this concept because pride can quickly erode your resilience efforts. Pride only searches for the why and always tries to place blame. In order to bounce back better, you need to do a thorough review of what part you potentially played in the matter. By doing this, you could avoid a duplicate occurrence.

Step back; let your sense of wonderment dream a new dream for you. Consider how you could benefit others with what you have gone through. Some of the greatest humanitarian efforts stemmed from people who stood up and stepped back in preparation of taking a step down. We continue to talk about them naturally because they stood out.

What step are you on right now?
How are you leveraging humility?
Who are you extending grace to?

What?	When?	How?	Skills?
Be Curious	Step One	Stand Up	Courage
Endure	Step Two	Step Down	Humility
	Step Three	Step Back	
Don't lose heart	Step Four	Stand Out	Capacity

CHAPTER 5

CONCLUSION

I f it had been possible for me to reach through time and comfort my past self, I would have repeatedly shouted, "wait until you see what comes from this."

My life has been greatly enriched by the stories and lessons I shared in this book. Today, I recognize had I not gone through the valley of despair in my past positions, I would not be qualified for my current profession in leadership development. When I was sitting at my former desk lamenting my current state, I would have never imagined the experience was going to be the defining moment of what the future held for me.

I did not know I would be called upon to help others, and those difficult days were the training ground for my future success. I continue to see the look of despair in the eyes of the many leaders I teach and hear the despair in their stories. I remember the pain of giving your best to people, only to find they won't deem it to be enough. Nowadays, I have the pleasure of sharing my resilience story with others in search of solutions. I can hold steady as they share their disappointments and surprise at the emotional turmoil accompanying leadership.

I can advise and coach them in the area of racial resilience and point them in the direction of healing. I can also educate them concerning the necessity of understanding the power derived from corporate resilience.

Every day, I have the distinct honor of being a bra to someone in need of support.

The image of who I thought I was faced incessant scrutiny.

From the newborn me, bruised, hairy and naked in all of my glory, bursting on the scene, to the six-year-old me refusing to face the flames by running and hiding rather than braving the bitter cold that comes from a season of winter.

The teenage me, sitting in the church pew, unwanted and rejected, pondering what God's love and acceptance really looks like.

The military me, attempting to blend into an unfamiliar structure, only to discover even camouflage could not make my race invisible.

The resilient me, acquiring what I believed was bulletproof attire— only to have it fail to protect me when I needed it the most.

The broken me, longing for the sorrow to fade quicker than it did, only to find that a river of tears feeds into an ocean of opportunity.

These were only a few of my defining bootstrap moments, when I decided to lace up my boots and continue to walk. I did not always know if I was headed in the right direction, but I believed the path I was on would eventually take me where I was supposed to be.

* * *

Now, in place of who I wanted people to think I was, is my authentic self.

I no longer let others' perceptions or preconceived notions of who I am hold me hostage and you shouldn't either. You need to take a good look at yourself, dig deep, pull hard on the bootstrap and get moving on the road ahead of you. You can determine your next steps.

Daily, I have the pleasure of helping others to heal from the organizational and personal wounds inflicted upon them. I would not have been suited for this work if I had not been through the recovery process myself. This required me to take an exhaustive inventory of my wounds and scars, because we treat each of them differently.

There were days I could barely find my boots, more less worry about pulling them up.

While I do not know what the future holds for me, I continue to wake up every day knowing I can weather whatever storm I face. I am convinced of this because of my past failure and success. I remained standing when life tried really hard to knock me down. If I had known the purpose of intentional resilience was to serve as a reminder of what I could achieve, I would have paid closer attention to the sights and sounds of my life's journey. I would have a playlist of the inspirational music, so I could play it again at a future date. I would have carefully catalogued the weapons which defeated my enemies and the ones which left me with self-inflicted wounds. Don't miss a moment, create a daily journal to capture your insights, melodies, thoughts, and reflections. This type of resilience requires you to live in the present. Embrace it.

Finally, I am passionate about sharing the peace I gained by leveraging spiritual resilience. I am convinced the hand of God has directed and protected me, right from the time I was growing in my mother's womb. This began with her choice to have and raise me. I have a purpose for being alive on this planet, at this time in history, and I will fulfill it in order to honor the God I serve. I believe this is the truth and the guiding principle of my existence. I can triumph over adversity, because there are many who have already shown me the way to do this.

All we need to do is to follow the yellow brick road.

There are many roads left behind by others who walked the path before you. It is unwise to negate all the historical wisdom passed down from past generations. Have you considered how, 200 years ago, someone experienced a situation very similar to yours and yet you are struggling for the solution here and now?

It doesn't matter if their insult was verbal and yours came by way of the internet.

Pain has a way of isolating us and making us think we are the only ones who ever felt the way we do. This is a fallacy; millions of people before us hurt and many of those around us are currently hurting. Connecting to them, their faith or their stories is one way we can move past our emotions.

In acknowledging you are not alone, you will begin to see clearer and before long, you will find strength from this new knowledge. Exploring how others' faith assisted them, helps us to redesign our next steps. When I read stories about people in similar situations and how they handled them, I was amazed at some of the new ideas I gained.

When I realized and accepted God's love, everything in my life changed. Realizing He was for me and not against me made me see myself differently. Self-reliance became a thing of the past when I realized I could trust the biblical promises. This morning, coming out of the clouds and hovering over the ocean, I witnessed a rainbow. In the Christian tradition, this is God's way of letting his people know that He is a promise keeper. I share this to tell you that the rainbow itself is a symbol of spiritual resilience, simply giving believers permission to continue to believe and to hope for the things God has promised despite their current circumstances.

It is no mistake I saw the rainbow today as I wrote down my final thoughts.

This book is a promise fulfilled, and a testament to corporate, intentional, and spiritual resilience.

The bras in our lives are undeniably vital yet not always available.

Your bootstraps are always available but not always advisable or appropriate.

The above two points are why I suggest considering the Bible as a first resort instead of the last. Spiritual resilience provides you with an unlimited supply of power to bounce back, always available, always appropriate. Take time to consider the ways in which you could benefit from all three types of resilience. You owe it to yourself to explore them.

I hope you have found this information useful and it will benefit you as you progress to your next level of resilience.

Made in the USA
Middletown, DE
10 January 2023